Meetings
with
Remarkable
Animals

Jaiia Earthschild

This book is dedicated to

Eve Downs

Nov 19 1925 - Jan 12 2018

My Remarkable Mother

A true Animal Whisperer
whose last wish was to

"...teach people to be kind..."

Content

1	Introduction	1
2	Song Medicine - Preface (sort of)	9
3	Treestory	20
4	Once upon an Earth Day	37
5	Aumakua	44
6	Parrot Tails	49
7	Bee-attitudes	66
8	Arach-needs	77
9	The Joyful Mystery School	90
10	Bird Mother	103
11	Close Encounters of the Fish Kind	115
12	The Possum Prince	122
13	A Truly Remarkable Mammal	129
14	The Shadow & the Warriors of Peace	132
15	Acknowledgements	141
16	Endnotes (some are stories)	144

Introduction

In titling this book *Meetings With Remarkable Animals*[i] I owe Gurdjieff (author of 'Meetings with Remarkable Men') at least the respect of acknowledgement. He and I are birthday neighbours although to be honest, in spite of his immense personal strength and force of character, I hope that we do not share too many other traits. But our books share certain qualities. Gurdjieff uses his connections with men he loves and respects as learning tools for his own evolution and conscious development and I have done the same with animals.

This little book contains a collection of true stories about voluntary connections with wild creatures; experiences that have humbled me and nourished me deeply; moments when animals have taught me in unique and wonderful ways, things that I would never have learned from a book or another human.

Apart from choosing to swim in a bay where dolphins are known to hang out with humans, all of these interactions have occurred spontaneously in or close to the animals' natural habitats. They have been with creatures as small as bees and as vast as the leviathans of the deep.

Each of these moments has inspired me to awe – or wonder - a quality of emotion almost lost in our jaded time; one that is said by Rudolf Steiner to be essential if we wish to awaken our perception to dimensions which exist outside our normal every day awareness.

As quantum physics reveals the mysteries of the sub-atomic world where wave can become particle and particle becomes wave in a universe that is blinking in and out of what we precariously cling to as 'reality', the separation between 'spirit' and 'matter' blurs and dissolves. Think of how much of what we experience is essentially wave-like: our thoughts, our feelings, music, breath, in fact the entire gestalt of consciousness could be defined as 'wave energy' and yet it is all connected to and interacting with what we accept as the physical reality of our lives. Most religions at core are containers for those very thoughts and emotions, values etc. shaping them so that we will live our lives together in some semblance of kindness and relative peace. Clearly a few of them have succeeded for a few of their members, but since they have been as much a part of civilization as fire and housing, we can only speculate on how humanity might have evolved without its religions.

The Dalai Lama says that ours is becoming a secular society and perhaps we are growing beyond the need for the spiritual support systems which over millennia have acted as intermediaries between the people and inspired truth. 'Spirituality is man's relationship with the divine,' was posted recently on Facebook, 'religion is crowd control'. Spirare is the Latin root of *spirit*. It means to breathe. To *inspire* is to breathe in; to *expire* (to breathe out) is to die…so…

> *what is the purpose of all this air that we respire,*
> *as we aspire to inspire*
> *before we expire?*

Well, the air to some great extent comes from the trees; from the plant world; from a benevolent Nature that requires no words; no beliefs; no priests; no temple walls. A unique blue-green planet warmed and lit by a burning star that is mathemagically situated to support the enigma that is life on earth. A gardener, a mountain climber, a bushwalker, a surfer – whoever spends time in close relationship with the natural world uncovers personal mysteries and unique soul nourishment with a language all its own.

And where nature is still this self-existing temple it is my experience that the animals living freely there will at times play the roles of priest or priestess, (if that is how I choose to perceive it) initiating me innocently, without ever intruding upon my personal power or my own numinous connection with the vastness. Invariably, once the moment is complete, they return to their own business completely disinterested in me or my future.

Ever since we as a species succumbed to the lie of scarcity economics, spiritual teachers have, as a matter of survival, needed to make enlightenment difficult for their students to achieve. Whereas, given their own natural habitat, what healthy animal needs or wants a human to provide for it?

Enlightenment is our birthright, as free and as essential as the air, land and clean water that until recently provided us with an abundance of fresh organic food minus any dependence upon corporate agri-business. Throughout my life whilst attempting to reclaim that birthright, I have focused on the sources and the solutions for environmental issues and have found myself walking almost involuntarily on a parallel path where sexuality – from courtship to conception, birth, parenting, education and beyond, mirrors our relationship to the mother planet upon which we depend. If we hope to become effective stewards or even to remain ongoing participants in the biosphere which we have almost destroyed, it is critical for humanity to learn to respect how we as a species co-create and sustain life and to share that respect with all the co-existing forms of life that make up our world family. In short, good parenting and healthy family life is utterly crucial to harmonious life on earth.

Just as we - unconsciously or consciously - long for truly life-enhancing sexuality, we also long for connectedness to the other species with whom we share this planet. Which might explain the ubiquity of both pornography and cute cat videos on the web. Until we get ourselves back into balance with our own sacred animal nature and the sacred nature of animals, we will exploit our sexuality as brutally as we exploit the animals.

Unbalanced and unfulfillable, our obsessive cravings diminish our personal power and harm others.

No matter how sophisticated we become, we have yet to find another life-support system or to build anything remotely like this one. And that is true whether we believe that we have only one shot at life on earth and therefore are trying to preserve it for our offspring or we believe along with billions of others in reincarnation. Not much to look forward to in the way of either fortunate grandchildren or fortunate rebirth if the nest is uninhabitable...

So it must be about the right time for us to learn to live harmoniously on this our only home in the known universe..

"Listen to the animals; for if you listen, they will teach you." (Native American wisdom)

Well to start with, the only animals I have ever seen who were not phenomenal parents, were either industrialized or abused - these two seem to go hand in hand, so we who have unleashed for ourselves a pandemic of broken and dysfunctional families could possibly learn a thing or two right there. But that is only the beginning.

People have been having wonderful interactions with animals for as long as we've all been sharing the same world. Somehow we have suppressed this vital part of our soul life, or compressed it - confining it to our own special dog or cat or caged budgie whilst ignoring the plight of literally billions of animals raised and killed in unspeakable circumstances for the global meat markets. Statistics clearly show that if we all merely halved our consumption of animal products it would massively reduce virtually every single one of our planetary stresses and most of our human illnesses. I am not suggesting that we all become total vegans overnight. But it is my dream to live in a world where along with our growing compassion towards our fellow humans, we become genuinely respectful and humane in our treatment of animals, domestic or wild. They are our family. How we treat them is critical to our own health and happiness. I am reminded of Temple Grandin, a true autistic avatar who overcame her own enormous personal and social challenges and went on to design systems within the beef industry of the USA that dramatically reduced animal suffering. Her work transcends the ideological battles between carnivores and vegans (between which I have frequently found myself sandwiched whilst formulating this book). Grandin thinks in pictures which is fundamental to inter-species communication. Her logic, re the animals bound for slaughterhouses: (paraphrased from the film based on her life and work) "If we did not eat them, we would not breed them so they wouldn't have life at all. But since we do, the least we can do is to treat them with respect."

It is not my intention to speak of the animal cruelty that is pervasive worldwide in any detail in this book. I know it exists and I know that it has to be dealt with, (*see chapter 13*) but I am consciously choosing to uplift our perceptions about life. The media is filled with reasons for despair. I believe that as we grow to recognise and respect the consciousness of the creatures around us, we have already begun a worldwide movement that refuses to allow their abuse to continue. I do however invite each of you to become aware of our treatment of animals. Sign those petitions and look very carefully at how you vote with your dollars, not to mention with your digestive system. Whatever one's beliefs, compassion is an inevitable symptom of increased consciousness. The suffering of innocence in any species, human or animal, is our own shared suffering. As long as we live with daily denials – whether of the pain that goes on behind the food that we eat or the domestic violence that plagues every suburb, we also then disconnect ourselves from the significance and the privilege that it is to participate in the life of this planet. We are responsible, we are not to blame. I invite us all to play our parts in the transformation of how we treat this exquisite blue-green jewel while it still shines in the vastness we like to call heaven. All cosmological studies and searches so far suggest that it is unique. So let's make the best of living on an absolute miracle while we have the opportunity.

Many years ago, whilst touring a series of concerts dedicated to the living earth, I was invited to 'edutain' about 100 children in a Rudolf Steiner (Waldorf) School in Adelaide, South Australia. The kids ranged in age from about 7 to 18. It was quite a moment to see them in a huge circle, all looking to me to keep their afternoon interesting. I remember we shared some songs and some lively acoustic games, and then I told them the true story of the humpback whales and the native Hawaiian sandalwood trees (Chapter 1, Treestory,). Not a cough and barely a movement interrupted us in that room for the better part of 45 minutes. After the day was done I left the main office and was heading off down the street with my arms full of instruments. A child of about eight was following me, desperately trying to get my attention. The story had changed her worldview completely. She had to ask me if it was REALLY true. I was able to look her in the eye and assure her that it was not a fairy tale at all and that every word was not only true but my own personal experience. She begged me not to leave. She told me it was the most important thing she had ever heard. I hope that she, who must now be an adult, finds this book. If you do, thank you. You inspired me to document these special and sacred interactions.

Perhaps these tales will stir your own memories. If you have stories that you are willing to share please contact me via the website. But I make a heartfelt request that the tales are true and not exaggerated or fabricated in any way. I am all for myths and legends; they are an extremely important part of a healthy culture, but what I am documenting here is not that. There is a genuine magic that exists on our earth and it needs no fantasy to improve it.

Thank you for your time and attention. It is now my great pleasure to share with you some meetings with some of the remarkable animals with whom we are sharing a truly remarkable planet…

2 ~ Song Medicine (a sort of preface)

Apparently infant arias wafted from the cot where, on the spurious advice of a certain Dr Spock (who later apologised for his mistake) I was one of a slew of infants left for long hours to their own devices; Song was my first comforter and although I have no memory of it, they say that I sang my first connected sentence. Some years later, having survived seven schools on two continents as an incurable misfit, this left-handed English protestant landed in an Australian Catholic school and began formal music training. I was fortunate to be placed in a unique choir; one of a handful of bewildered schoolgirls tucked amidst rows of nuns, monks, a few priests-in-training and a collection of minuscule choirboys. Although this touring choir, *The Singers of David,* was run with all the patriarchal and hierarchical pomp for which the Roman church is renowned, Sister Mary Gabriel, my convent music teacher, was in fact the power behind the music throne. A large moon-faced woman, her pleasantly phlegmatic air masked the most brilliantly staged one-woman feminist revolution that I have been privileged to witness. As queen of Sydney's Catholic music world she held court in the convent, far from the mundanities of the school proper. She somehow remained free of the usual constraints that have shackled nuns since convents were first invented. Before her, maybe only Hildegard von Bingen and a few retired queens in the Middle Ages lived so autonomously wearing the habit of a nun. Completely unconcerned by my various non-Catholic handicaps, Sister Gabriel liked my voice and therefore quite miraculously salvaged my soul, not necessarily from hell but definitely from an earthly future minus any hope of self-esteem. Under her tutelage I sang amidst the clergy in the cathedrals and country town halls of eastern Australia, on weekly television and once (the morning after a local debut as the witch in 'Bell Book and Candle' - hair dyed a very pagan shade of black with a long silver streak) I sang with this extraordinary choir for the pope. I remember watching the indomitable Sister Gabriel waltzing gracefully at midnight in a nightclub, in the far north of Queensland, blissfully recalling her pre-convent days as the belle of Toowoomba, unfazed either by her enormous girth or her tropical full length robes. She taught me something about the liberating power of music that went beyond the notes on the manuscripts or even the magic of the multi-phonic voicestra that was the gift of my high school years.

Life had presented me with some early challenges. Music gave me strength. It was not that I was a great musician or that I had a remarkable voice; music was my friend; not to mention my therapist. Practising Bach preludes and fugues literally reconfigured my confused brain. Although I am sure I never played as Bach would have wished, I could feel the orderly mathematical forms soothing the inner chaos. And singing was a transcendent mystery that permeated my traumatized adolescent body and made it possible to survive an unknowable past until I was old enough to deal with it consciously. Our personal demons, once owned and embraced truly do become significant allies, often bringing gifts for others that we meet along the way. Intuitively I found a path of healing long before I realised that I needed one.

Song medicine part 2
I pursued music as a vocation but after a year at the state Conservatory I found the politics in those hallowed halls were diminishing my love for the art. It was amongst Rudolf Steiner's acolytes, while training as a music therapist that I became conscious of the healing qualities of sound.
I worked for several years amongst children whose bodies could not or would not express themselves as most of ours do. For them it was often revelatory to have someone match their sounds, their tones, their drum beats or their bodily rhythms. By surrendering my apparent knowledge and by meeting each being in their expressive comfort zone, we were together able to reach hitherto locked arenas of communication. This principle became foundational to the interspecies communion that has become such a meaningful part of this life. The children I apparently

'taught' were my teachers. At times I witnessed flashes of genius emergent from minds and bodies that society had deemed uneducable. Through those 'autistic avatars' and 'idiot savants' I learned to be wary of the human centred hubris which denies all forms of intelligence that it cannot quantify or regulate. Those unconditionable children and young adults also helped me to liberate myself from the printed music score to which I had chained myself by years of classical training. Rudimentary improvisations for extraordinarily creative movement therapy sessions and simple compositions for whatever voices and instruments the close-knit team of teachers and therapists were willing to explore evolved into delightful weekly concerts and seasonal celebrations. This was the birthing ground for the songs, musicals and rock opera that I have since created. At a time when women were not encouraged to become composers, our warmly appreciative and completely non-judgemental audience was a precious gift.

Although I play several instruments, I would say that in the therapeutic realm only the drum, the didgeridoo and the violin (none of which I play) come near to the versatility and subtlety of the human voice. But in the hands of the heart, any tool can be transformative. In fact *not* knowing an instrument can level the playing field. I often used a drum in my years as a music therapist. I remember one child in particular was vastly more skilful than I was. His Greek folk soul was happy playing 11/17 rhythms while I with my Anglo-Celtic limitations could only watch in amazement. For him, this was thoroughly empowering.

Psychic Discoveries behind the Iron Curtain, written by Sheila Ostrander in 1970, was perhaps the first book in modern times to document the effect of different kinds of music on plant growth. Certain classical music was clearly a tonic and some heavy rock was definitely not. Masaru Emoto, in his ground-breaking photos of the crystalline formations of water also showed the immense difference between the effects of say, Beethoven and death metal. The latter might serve as a temporary catharsis for some, but not all music is beneficial for lasting health. Any potent medicine - even water - can be a poison depending on the dose. Should you be inspired to try out your skills as a sound healer, honour your own gifts and preferences, but stay humble; there is much to learn. Then listen to your heart and the hearts of those you are attempting to serve and try not to take yourself too seriously. This chapter is only an introduction to a realm that goes beyond the scope of this book. I will focus more on the power of vocal sound in a future volume.

Matching tone or vibration to mental, physical or emotional pain will usually transform the experience. That is probably why we shout and scream when we bang our toe or bump up against an adversary. But screaming quickly makes one's voice too raw to continue and shouting can frighten others away just when we most need to be understood. It is possible to find tones and chanted vibrations which go to the heart of the matter. One can then remain there until things shift without either antagonising the neighbours or blowing out one's throat chakra. One might call this 'sound empathy' although in earlier times it was often called 'enchantment'.

Religions use this latent power within the human voice for purposes of transcendence. Rudolf Steiner has said that the entire phenomenon of the Gothic cathedrals (into which over one third of the wealth of Europe was invested over centuries) was created intuitively to carry the sound of the harmony of the fifth which first entered into western consciousness at that time. I have been initiated into sacred seed syllables, mantras and tones of power, but I believe it is a mistake to grant exclusive sanctity to any one sound or system of sound. Attuned to personal power, one can access extraordinary sounds. It is a gift of our challenging era that we as individuals are capable of becoming our own priests and priestesses. The priestly intermediaries of religious belief systems often dilute the direct experience of the numinous which most of us yearn for at times in our lives. The unknowable has revealed itself to me through nature in ways that have changed my life. I cannot say that of the countless experiences I have had in churches and temples although I recognise and respect that much of the finest architecture and music throughout human endeavour has been created for the worship of that which we call God .

I worked for over a decade as a musician and sound therapist amongst teachers of conscious sexuality (otherwise known as western Tantra). Although it is an energy that has been deeply supressed and / or exploited, loving sexuality can be a direct path to personal awakening. Much of the work we did was directed towards the healing of the dysfunctional overlays of shame and violation that have been generated by centuries of repression. This is a complex issue and one which I address in other books.[ii] Sound was integral to the seminars and to our research. Abuses of the body mind cannot be healed through the intellect alone. Where there is tissue trauma as is almost always the case in sexual wounding, sound is a critical part of the healing process. I see the healing of human sexuality as integral to the healing of our biosphere. Perhaps interspecies communion begins with building understanding between the mysterious polarities of man and woman.

When I wish to make contact with a being of any species, I allow their world to play upon my consciousness enough that I might respectfully attempt to echo or mirror them with body language, mood or sound. I cannot emphasize enough that one has to listen with one's entire being. At times I have been arrogant, putting in my two cents worth too soon only to watch a wild creature scuttle off in disgust or well-founded fear. But when one is calmly present and coming from a quietly open heart, animals tend to be forgiving of imperfections in accent or tone. Which is fortunate as it is no mean feat to accurately echo a bird or a bee or a dolphin. Often they respond to honest song. I remember the first time I ever saw wild deer in California. Two of them were moving along the side of a small gulch across from where I was standing, apparently oblivious to my presence. I very softly began to sing. They froze and rather touchingly hid behind a couple of narrow trees; meaning that they tucked their heads behind the trees, leaving their bodies fully exposed. One by one, they peeked out to look at me, too curious of the song to remain in their woefully inadequate hiding places. Peek-a-boo with deer; for me it was love at first sight - while they did the listening. I have never yet made a decent deer sound, having only ever heard them in the distance.

It is important to note here that song is for me a communion from the heart. (With all due respect to the fine art of opera, if I were to bellow like a tenor about to commit suicide in the last act of a grand opera, I am pretty sure that most animals would give me a wide berth. Many people commune telepathically with animals in apparent silence. There is more than one way to bridge the so-called language gap. Thinking in pictures is a critical tool when communing with animals but only after you have their attention and trust. For me song has frequently been a great way to introduce myself to another species. Music really is a universal language. One just has to be sensitive as to what kind of music, how loud and when. Timing, if not everything, is certainly a lot…

Of all the creatures that I have encountered, the birds and the cetaceans are so sound oriented that they often seem as fascinated by my sound as I am by theirs, especially when I am playful and unself-conscious. Those that are not extinct seem to have survived largely through being wary of the speaking tones of us two footed creatures and yet nearby birds often seem to listen when a human sings from the heart. Groups of different bird species will sometimes add choruses, catching beats, emphasizing spaces, trilling and generally singing along. At times it seems uncanny. But nature is like that.

I have learned with wounded birds that it almost always relaxes them if one sings very softly and gently, allowing the heart to choose sounds that might vibrate soothingly into their hollow-boned, delicate little bodies. There is still a listening quality to this; it is not a performance. One must attune carefully to the spirit of the bird and allow the sound to adapt to their need. Even if one has no idea what is their natural sound, this generally works. With birds it appears to be quite regularly miraculous. I know it is not. What some call magic is science that has yet to be discovered. But mystery is a tonic for us jaded humans, so until these kinds of sound healings are carefully quantified and documented, I will take the liberty of calling them magical – just know that I use the word lightly.
Amongst dolphins or whales in the wild I can be pretty robust. I have found myself making a – to put it euphemistically - eclectic collection of sounds which can seem anything from weird to thoroughly frightening to nearby humans – even me (!). But this has been a very effective way to attract the attention of cetaceans in the vastness of the ocean. (See *The Joyful Mystery School*) I would definitely not make such sounds near to a dolphinarium. To me such places feel like prisons or Victorian mental asylums; I am at a loss as to why or how they continue to exist. This book is about non-predatory animals in their chosen habitat. I have had very little experience with carnivores. I would not recommend that anyone start roaring at a lion or diving in to swim with orcas unless you already know them quite well! (*see 'A Truly Remarkable Mammal' P. 122*)

Whatever I have experienced with animals and sound, there are countless others who have phenomenal interactions. I am moved to document a few precious moments on behalf of the natural world which, although it communicates very clearly, is seldom heard or understood by humanity. Maybe this will inspire a few more of us to recognise our place amongst all beings; not as dominators but as family sharing one home. I know to some that will sound so new-age-tree-huggy-wuggy but trivialization is a tool that has been used by conquerors to overshadow the wisdom of indigenous peoples for centuries. Now we are giving greater respect to those who came before, whilst frequently mocking any of our own tribe who choose to share ancient values. That is okay with me. I have many times played the clown; from the white-faced mime variety to the fool-on-the-hill, I have been laughed at by cockatoos, parrots, dolphins cats and humans. It is a small step from humiliation to humility and from there to liberation. So please laugh! This planet needs it at least as much as I do.

It is my perception that now we need to sit up and take some serious notice of the billions of other sentient beings who vastly enrich our biosphere. They have a collective wisdom that spans hundreds of millions of years. Every creature that has shared its inner life with me has revealed qualities of soul and awareness that have delighted me, taught me and altered my worldview. I have learned from them that it is only through listening that we find authentic communion and that silence is the medium through which communication flows.

Perhaps what I have really learned
reflected back to me
from the souls of animals
is to hear the sound of one heart slowly illuminating.

3 ~ Treestory

Treestory? – Yes this is a living myth that includes trees – the native Hawaiian Sandalwoods that were brought almost to extinction – humans and the great humpback whales…spanning as it does at least 175 years, it will take a bit of historical prefacing, so make yourself a cup of your favourite brew, relax and enjoy the longest story in this little book of otherwise very short stories…

You see I'm a treestorian... you know, like historians, herstorians, theirstorians and ourstorians. Well trees have been used pretty much exclusively to write all those stories *on*, so in a way I'm attempting to return the favour.

One of the more dangerous myths of Judeo-Christian culture is (loosely) "… everything on the earth was put here for man's use and dominion". In fact that one phrase, despite the fact that I can't remember it and refuse to own a bible, may have been responsible for more ecological havoc than all the foraging of all the dinosaurs that ever walked the earth and believe me in those days the trees were quaking in their roots.

The bible, being the first printed book off the Gutenberg press, has a claim, rivalled only by all the Sunday newspapers of the last century combined, for pulling down more of the primeval architecture of nature in order to pass on disinformation, inaccuracies and grossly mistranslated mythology in the name of truth, than maybe any other publication in 'his' story. "It's almost as if The Bible was written by racist, sexist, homophobic, violently sexually frustrated men instead of a loving God. Weird!" [iii] To be fair to its origins, I suspect something got lost in translation over the centuries.

Civilized man has had a habit of decimating forests for quite some millennia; and it is a tribute to the awesome abundance of the planet that there are still any to cut. There are a few, very few... Four per cent of the old growth forest is left in the United States - at least that was last millennium's count. It may be down to three and a half... no... three ... now it's one...oh-oh...

Treestory Part 2

This is a story of 'The Fragrant Isles' as the Hawaiian Islands were once known to the whalers and the traders that visited in the late eighteenth and early nineteenth century. The scent of the sandalwood forests would waft across the oceans to the ships before land was sighted so it is told. Until the traders brought their fascinating wares to the ali'i (the island aristocracy) wanting riches in return.

Now sandalwood was and remains to this day one of the two most highly prized woods on earth. By around the year 1800, the *ali'i* were some $250,000 in debt (and that is a lot more then than I'm willing to even guess at on today's market). Quite naturally the *ali'i* wanted to become part of the new world. Guns, velvets, ships; entry into 'civilization' had a price then as now. There were no credit cards, only natural resources.

Now any developing country in our time could predict the next part of this tale; they who have experienced the benevolence of the World Bank or the International Monetary Fund. Great sums of money are lent and then the natural wealth is drained like so many pounds of flesh from country after country while the children in those lands get hungrier and hungrier. Where are the forests that once covered Nepal? The Sahara? Was it the Roman Empire that turned Northern Africa into desert? Who buys all that wood from Indonesia? And the Amazon? The story gets repeated time and time again. A land gets emptied of its forests, the rains go, the food goes, the fuel goes, the animals die and the people starve. Gradually, almost imperceptibly the oxygen replenishment for the entire planet is compromised. You know, don't you, that the forests are the lungs of the earth. Did you know that you breathe some 10 to 20 per cent less oxygen than your grandparents did? Did you ever consider that almost all diseases are exacerbated by lack of oxygen? One might consider planting trees as an alternative to health insurance...

Treestory Part 3

Until consumerism hit the islands, the trees had been cut only for sacred purposes - canoes, temple pillars and the like. And then they were cut amidst songs and ceremony and great respect.

But suddenly, the *maka'aina* (the people of the land – those who in Europe were called 'peasants' or 'serfs') were sent up the mountain to the cold and wet lands where for thirty years they toiled, until by 1830 every last sandalwood tree had been cut down and fitted into the hulls of ships bound for China. The *maka'aina* stamped out the seedlings. They longed to return to their village lifestyle in the warmer lands down by the coast and never again wanted to use their mana (life force) to raze forests.

They used up a lot of mana. Between 1830 and 1890 some three hundred thousand islanders died from introduced diseases. In 1895 the US government overthrew the monarchy of Hawaii, imprisoned the last reigning Hawaiian queen, Liliuokalani in her palace and illegally annexed the islands. Numerous factors in those equations, but I am haunted by the words of one *kumu* (teacher) on the Big Island when the last piece of native rainforest was fenced off for the building of a geothermal plant in the 1990's: "Death of a forest, death of a culture" he said; a man of knowledge; one who knew the healing plants; one who was steeped in the wisdom of the ancestors. Bear with me. The story is not all tragedy and gloom though it may well be one huge cautionary tale...

Treestory Part 4

Some 155 years later, one of God's clowns was hijacked (was it the druid ancestry?) from a more or less respectable life in a small coastal town in Australia, and was deposited one midnight at Kahului airport, Maui with about $100 and a few costume changes. Some accident of birth had combined the blood of a line of Welsh witches who might have fallen from the wrong side of Merlin's blanket with the Cook family of Northern

England (the explorers and travellers) but when I arrived late one night on Maui, I blissfully dropped my name and personal history at the airport and melted into the velvety sweetness of that hospitable and unequivocally magic island.

Within a year, I had also dropped all vestige of civilized living and found myself living very quietly and mostly naked on a beach, relatively far from the madding crowds, for several months. A lifelong concern for the ecological safety of the planet had led me to pursue a vision quest. Eating only when someone chose to offer food; not speaking much, but at times singing for the gods of the ocean and the land, mostly I just watched the stars spinning, the bombs falling on Kaho'olawe (a small island about a mile away that was used for decades as a target practice for the US military), and the waves crashing on the shore. After a few months my internal dialogue all but ceased. This is often a pre-condition for remarkable events to start taking over an otherwise ordinary life…and sure enough…

One starlit pre-dawn, I awoke aware that it was my 'birthday'. I had a devoted ally back in civilization who had insisted on leaving a car not far from where I slept so that I could be safe. I arose and, following the kinds of instincts that are to be found once the chatter of the mind is quiet, drove from the shore all the way up the mountain to its peak. In the icy darkness at 10,000 feet above sea level, I clothed myself in everything I could find in the car that might keep me warm and set off across the mountain top dressed in a collection of brilliant pink and turquoise oddments including striped leggings and a hat - the clown incarnate, stumbling towards infinity. Shortly before dawn I found myself running and leaping across the jagged mountain ridges as though guided by unseen hands. The lava

24

fields at the top of the mountain are no longer accessible to humanity, but in those days, the odd fool could pretty much go wherever their feet took them into a splendid isolation perhaps unmatched anywhere on earth given that the Hawaiian island chain is the farthest of all landmasses from any continent. Eventually I found myself sitting on a remarkably comfortable throne of ancient lava watching the sun rise over Haleakala and the distant peaks of Mauna Loa and Mauna Kea on the Big Island. Apparently alone, I drew out my sacred tobacco pipe offering a puff to the unseen Madam Pele, goddess of the volcanoes, who was at that time, one of my very few friends. A thin wisp of smoke rose from the pipe – breathed perhaps by the invisible lips of Pele? Ecstatically ignited by the majesty and the mystery I jumped up and began to dance in the pink and turquoise dawn. Spinning, I noticed the observatory windows glinting in the sun on the volcanic peak. Hundreds of visitors and tourists flock the mountain top each morning to watch the sunrise. They had themselves quite the spectacle that morning; the fool on the hill unwittingly costumed to match the sky.

Returning across the lava field in the early morning light, I discovered Pele's sculpture garden. Gnarled griffins rising in lava tinged with pink and mauve, vast winged birds and tiny creatures as complex and curious as the gargoyles on cathedral rooftops surrounded me. It was here that I first grasped why Pele's rocks have always been honoured by the Hawaiians as sacred. From the largest to the tiniest, it was as though each one had been formed to tell a story; whether mythical or imaginary this was altering my brainwaves as I walked. Thirsting I went down on my knees and found that I could draw icicles out of the loose lava gravel on the ground and these also were shaped into mythical forms that melted into my mouth fuelling the morning with mineral richness. This was turning into quite a birthday – and the sun had barely risen.

Every moment of that day was filled with marvels – the return journey down to the ocean; my solitary explorations amongst the lava tubes and hills that surround the beach where I was living; from heiau to heiau, (natural rock altars left by the early inhabitants of the islands) the day was an initiation into mysteries that can never be fully explained in words. All that can be done is to describe a part of the magic in the hope that others might one day dare to follow their heart's call and uncover the wonder that lives within each one of us.

By sunset I was no longer the girl I had once been – I was not even an individuality. I was one with the elements - an exquisite wave of gratitude and bliss that had temporarily abandoned its origins and future. The present was a truly a gift.

Thus primed, I was on the side of a rocky outcrop between two beaches as the sun began to sink behind Kaho'olawe, the island that was still being used as a bomb testing ground across the sea. I squatted down to pee. The sun was shining on the ocean in a golden path and it shone on the waters flowing from my body. "Pees on earth" I whispered and at that moment, a force overtook my entire being. I felt my body suddenly throbbing with a deep vibration that was barely audible as sound – much lower than any I could make. Rising, I who had sung since infancy and studied sound with mystics, classics and clans of many cultures, witnessed a soundscape emerging from my body that was like nothing I had ever experienced before. Every cell began to resonate – split tones, unstructured sounds that echoed and flowed without conscious interference. Simultaneously some 10 to 15 (I wasn't counting) whales began leaping and thrashing their tales in the direct line of the setting sun. For as long as the sound emerged, the whales danced until, as the sun disappeared, the sounds faded away and the last few tails of the whales disappeared with what seemed like fond farewell waves beneath the sea.

I walked back to the sandy hillock where I usually slept. One man – another western sadhu disguised as a beach bum who had spent the better part of a year swinging in a hammock between two tiny trees – had distantly observed this phenomenon, which later proved to be a relief as otherwise I might never have believed that it had really happened. At the time, my brainwaves were so overwhelmed and altered that thought had disappeared. Inevitably it would return and try to make some sense of all this. But even now, writing almost a quarter of a century later, the mystery is greater than my mind's ability to comprehend it. What I did soon recall was one of my more magnificent mentors in sound, a woman small in stature yet vast in presence. Named 'Mechtild' (mighty maiden) by Rudolf Steiner as she sat on his knees as an infant; in adulthood she intimidated all who came into her aura, especially her students. This great woman had a profound and affectionate influence on me in my late teens. She had told me once: "When every cell resonates with sound, instant manifestation can take place." This is what is meant by 'casting a spell'. When we spell out our words with uninhibited personal power, extraordinary results ensue.

On this particular day, it was not the personality who did the spelling. I never did claim to 'channel' the whales – how could one so small hope to contain the consciousness of creatures so vast? It was they who had called me – or perhaps it was existence itself, in one spectacular moment of synchronicity. A man who had spent time with whales later suggested that when those vibrations filled my body, the cetaceans had entered me with their sonar, 'scoping me out' so to speak. It was over ten years before I began to grasp the full significance of it all.

Treestory part 5

I was dreadfully scrawny by now; and hadn't looked in a mirror for months. More than a little eccentric, very few humans were willing to talk with me. Isolated from my own kind, I kept returning to the shore to sing with those amazing animals with whom I felt deep kinship. Although never again were so many whales to leap up at one time, each time I sang or sounded at least one and often several whales seemed to get really excited and so did I. The sounds arose from within as if from the ocean itself. When people asked me to call the whales, I had to tell them that I could not; it was the whales who called me. At times I would throw off what few clothes I was wearing and dive into the ocean, swimming out fearlessly to depths and distances that at other times I have found thoroughly intimidating. (See Chapter 7, The Joyful Mystery School) I spent an entire winter this way, until in the spring, the whales left for their northern feeding grounds.

The ocean seemed unbearably empty. I left the beach and was drawn up to live in the mountain heights where, still sleeping outdoors, I walked the dry crackly landscape by day, listening for I did not know quite what. I found companionship in nature as most of humanity was still giving me a wide berth. As I walked amongst the scrub my legs felt drained and exhausted. I noticed that here so far from civilization, the landowners tended to feud amongst themselves. It was as though there was a disturbance in the land itself. Gradually a murmur emerged as if from the parched landscape:. "Give me back my forests." Forests? Surely this was relatively new lava and these spindly, prickly bushes were the first things to grow here... "Give me back my forests. Get the children to help. It will heal their spirits".

Now I might have looked wild but I had once been a scholar, so I took myself to the libraries and uncovered the sad story of the sandalwoods. I sensed that my days in the wilderness were over. Armed with a vision, I returned slowly and with great difficulty, to the world of humanity.

Three years passed until I was once again by the shore not far from where the whales had danced with me. I shared the tale at a long night fire and the story was then retold by others until by morning it had touched a modern day Johnny Appleseed. An ex-marine with a slightly fanatical gleam in his eyes, he was arguably the most appalling poet in the entire island chain – at least in the English language. He was also the being gifted by who knows what star, with the inspiration and dedication required to restore the native sandalwoods from the brink of extinction. He disappeared up the mountain and returned with the news that the rangers knew of a few old sandalwood trees and that if he wanted to try and get seeds to grow, he was welcome to them.

High up on the mountainside, hidden behind locked gates, the Sandalwood Man, as he liked to call himself, found the old trees and gathered some rat-eaten, mouldy looking seeds that were scattered beneath a couple of trees which looked as one might expect survivors of genocide to look: gnarled and twisted and covered in long strands of pale grey lichen that looked like the hair of witches in some tropical Shakespearean tragedy. He brought the seeds down the mountain along with a bag of sandalwood fruit which is reddish and rather like coffee berry. So began the era of the 'gypsy baby forest'. A motley group of activists began doing whatever they thought might help the seeds to germinate. This included everything from stomping on the berries and dying clothes with the juices, singing over the seeds, offering them menstrual blood tea and generally praying to whatever forces were considered to be beneficial to orphan trees. As luck would have it they did also plant the seeds in soil and began taking seed trays to various parts of the island to see where they might thrive. Logic being what it is, the Sandalwood man soon realized that since the survivors lived far above sea level, it was likely that the babies would like it there too. Someone offered him and his wife the use of a piece of land that was accessible by an almost impassable, rock strewn, jeep shattering stretch of what was euphemistically called a 'road' near the top of which was what was optimistically called a 'cottage'. The gypsy tree tribe set up camp. Adding a tipi, they were grateful for what comforts the cottage offered. It did have running water, managed to keep out at least most of the rain, and provided shade in the summer. It took over a year for a few seeds to germinate. They had, poor things, been dragged all around the island which despite its tiny size has 21 of the possible 23 meteorological zones on the planet. Amongst these many micro-climates, the sandalwoods turned out to be quite particular: they live above 2000 ft., not jungle (wet) side, and always close to Koa or other nitrogen fixing trees. The sandalwood is a social tree. It does not like to grow all alone.

By the next year, seed gathering was a group affair, with families and kids all traipsing up the long harsh roads to where the mother tree was hidden. When they arrived, they found a miracle. While the tribe was trying to get sad old seeds to germinate, over one hundred seedlings had sprouted under the mother tree. Given that not one had been there the year before, one could only assume that the original tree had somehow been invigorated by the sincere if misguided attentions of the tribe. In quantum physics there is a theory of entanglement – Einstein called it 'spooky theory'- where atoms that have been closely intertwined and then separated, will respond instantaneously to changes within one set of the atoms, even if they are hundreds of miles apart. The tribe watered and sang and danced and generally offered loving attention to the stressed and virtually barren seeds and that year the mother tree gave birth to new and viable seedlings; possibly for the first time in over one hundred and fifty years. Go figure…you might find a more logical explanation, but I'll stick with Einstein. Spooky!

It took some seven years for the Sandalwood Man with precious little help from others apart from his indomitably wild outlaw of a wife, to grow some forty thousand baby trees. He gave them away on the road sides. He planted them on ranch lands where the land owners agreed to fence them off from the feral pigs, goats and deer. Rarely did he sell a few and he could barely keep his family fed throughout these years. But some acres up in Poli-Poli state forest were fenced off and with the help of 'The Earth Guardians', a group of rap singing Maui teens, the tribe cleared away all the non-native plants from a little grove and planted several hundred trees back on the mountain where they were protected by (and from) the introduced redwoods which dominated the area up near the tree line. There was little water available so a drip system was attached to a tiny tank run by a solar panel and a minute wind generator which helped to provide sustenance.

Now perhaps I should reveal to you a little of the dark side of this story – why not? It's all history by now. One would think that everyone would be delighted to see the native trees back on the 'aina (the nourishing land). But this business of replanting was a less than popular venture amongst various of the island powers. The international developers and hoteliers who have grown immeasurably rich from placing their tourist ghettos in places where the sun always shines were not enthused by the prospect of returning forests to the mountain. Why? Well 150 years ago the rainfall above Kihei was about 100 inches a year. Deforestation did on Maui what it does the world over: It turned lush land into desert. But this has been good for tourism. Who wants to pay for a vacation where it's likely to rain? So, with many council members traditionally dwelling in the pockets of the developers, it was virtually impossible to get any assistance for these projects back then. To be fair to all, I believe that things have improved since for all things indigenous, including native reforestation.

Our Sandalwood man and his band of outlaws were not the most socially sensitive folk ever to land on the Hawaiian Islands – not the least either if one compares them to the missionaries and their offspring – but somehow they managed to incur the ire of some locals. This was brought home to me one morning when I answered a knock on the door where I was staying. A couple of local Hawaiian guys that I knew a bit from trips into the mountains were standing there. Although friendly enough as is the Hawaiian way, they delivered a warning: "If dat guy keeps plantin' dose trees da way he is, he gonna get a bullet tru him – you bettah tell 'im. It's not da local way OK?" A little taken aback by this early morning greeting, I managed to remember my roots as a daughter of Gaia, mother earth and responded by pointing out that worldwide more forests are being cut than are being planted and that since the forests were there long before the locals, perhaps the trees were not being replaced as a people pleaser, but to serve the land itself. The wiry old paniolo (cowboy) seemed to accept the logic of this, tipped his hat to me and very politely left. A death threat with aloha! Fortunately that was the end of it; so far no one has died on this particular quest.

Treestory part 6

I travelled long and far singing on behalf of the earth until one day I returned to the place where the whales had danced with me ten years earlier. Na Kupuna O Maui (the elders of the island) had gathered there to acknowledge that an American president (Clinton) had at last apologized for the coup that had illegally annexed the islands one hundred years earlier. As I sat down at the back of the tent, one of the elders was speaking about the *Kumu Lipo* - the Hawaiian chant of creation; which describes how each creature of the sea came into being with a creature or plant of the islands; the periwinkle with a certain fern, the rainbow fish with a special flower etc. "Of course," said he, knowing nothing of me or my journey, "the whales came into the world with the sandalwoods."
Suddenly all the pieces of my mythic journey fell gently into place. Actually it was never *my* journey. I had, by offering my services to the earth, played the part of a messenger and had been given the gift, as a poet and a visionary, of watching a

natural mystery unfold. I just happened to show up in time to hear him say those magic words.

Treestory part 7

That was many years ago. Since then, the sandalwood man has moved to the Big Island where older, wiser and more diplomatically correct, he continues planting native trees. The Maui sandalwoods have had to fend for themselves through drought, fire and landslides. Poli-Poli forest was closed for long seasons. I had to wait till the forest was reopened. Then having donned some sacred beads, and a necklace of puka shells to honour the whales, I walked the grove. Not a tree could I find. I searched and searched, weeping for the impotent littleness of being human. At the top of the fence line as I scraped by a bush, my beads dissolved in a cascade to the forest floor. These were the bones of my ancestors – the last gift of a beloved sister as she passed from this world. I fell to my knees and began a search that lasted an hour in the forest debris. As I scrabbled in the loose earth, I prayed - for the ancestors, for the unborn and for the baby trees I could not find. At that moment the shell necklace also broke from my neck – *pukas* falling into the ground. Now almost everybody who has ever visited Hawaii knows how Pele feels about stones, I more than many (but that is another story), so I started to take note of the cosmic message service that was screaming in my ear. Digging as I had through the grasses and undergrowth, I had cleared a sizeable space and looking closely it suddenly dawned on me that the skinny little stick growing laboriously through right angles and almost crushed by the weeds I had just inadvertently cleared was in fact a sandalwood baby. An infant not planted by human hands; nowhere near the irrigation systems. After that I found eleven really healthy, happy sandalwood teenagers that had been planted a few years earlier. They had survived drought and fire and had somehow given birth to one wild child.

It took thirty years to cut down the sandalwood forests. It took ten years for one tree to seed itself naturally on the mountain. A forest is more than a handful of trees. It is a whole lot easier to keep them on the land than it is to replace them once they are gone. Ditto whales, snow leopards, indigenous tribes and... humanity?

I am not sure that we humans can ever truly replace a forest but we can definitely plant trees. Maybe centuries from now, a whole new ecosystem will have established itself and who then will know how it all began?

Once
There were no islands
Then fields of rolling fire were cooled by endless seasons

The spirits sang
the mountains rang and answered
to life's desire

Once - In the mountains
Tiny seeds and spores began to cover the land
The spirits sang
the mountains rang and answered
to life's desire

Life of a woman – life of a man
Smaller than a century's span
What is our hunger? Can it be fed
Before the ancient wilderness is dead?

Now – now in the mountains
The hunger has a different sound –
cries to us from naked ground:
'Do you remember how sunlight weaves
mist and moss and forest leaves?'

Will you come with me to the land now bare?
And with this human hunger dare

to recreate the land
Seed by seed hand in hand
Recreate the land.
The precious land

4 ~ Once upon an Earth day...

Sometime around 1996, having taken reluctant note of a small insistent voice tugging at my inner sleeve, I found myself hosting a free concert on the stage of the Queen Kaahumanu Shopping Centre on Maui. This place has its architectural appeal with high-tensile open roofs that look like big white sails and can be adapted to the prevailing weather, giving an expansive open air feel to what would otherwise be your traditional shopping mall. Adding to its charm is a larger than life-sized statue of Queen Kaahumanu herself facing the stage and generally resplendent in fresh flower leis. This particular Hawaiian queen was responsible for breaking the long standing kapu (taboo) against women eating bananas in traditional Hawaiian culture. I invite you to use your imagination as to why the men might have found this threatening enough to create a life or death kapu that lasted for generations. In fact, some still blame the queen's gustatory rebellion for the subsequent influx of white people which lead to the almost total destruction of the Hawaiian people and their culture for several generations. Fortunately, the Polynesians being a powerful bunch, the culture has re-instated itself in recent decades and is now flourishing with renewed vigour. Many of the children speak the traditional language better than did their own parents or grandparents; and hula, the ancient genealogical chants, traditional stories, tapa making, ancient fishing and canoe practises are all lovingly cherished once again. The people are reawakening to a sense of their unique magnificence (with a little help from Bob Marley). Being somewhat of a maverick myself, the Queen's hefty presence in the midst of the consumer marketplace encouraged me to overcome my doubts about the wisdom of such an event in such a spot. I do like to listen to my inner voice; I just have some difficulty in being able to always tell the difference between wise guidance and pure mischief making on the part of my unconscious. I encourage you to adopt some of this healthy scepticism yourself should you ever embark upon the path of the magical. It does not make life easier but it will spare you from some embarrassing or possibly dangerous moments.

Anyway, this time in spite of the fact that the annual Maui Whale Day event was to take place on that same afternoon, I followed the voice. As musicians were tuning up I was inevitably running around dealing with technicalities. The downside of leadership when one is also a performer is that there is never any time to be the diva. My ex-husband and good friend the Wiz was running the sound board that day; he walked up to me with his hand closed saying 'Happy Anniversary" as he handed over something small and soft. Oh that's right, I thought as I juggled cords and speaker cables to receive his offering, we married on Earth Day. Opening my hand I found a wounded sparrow lying on its back with its claws in the air, its little beak open and gasping. The Wiz knew me well enough to know that this might take precedence over concert technicalities – well, sort of. I found myself attempting to deal with wires and microphones one-handed and by the time I was in the upstairs bathrooms trying to apply lipstick and sort out my hair, I was saying to the pathetic little thing clutched in my palm 'Sorry tiny one, I can only do so much for you right now, but I will love you the best I can…" It did not look as if there was much hope for it at this point. It looked dreadful. The concert began, Jaiia, bird in hand, improvising the introduction as usual:

"Happy Earth Day! Look, I have this wounded bird in my hand. It reminds me of our planet. If I hold it too tightly, I will crush it. If I do not hold it carefully it will fall to the ground and die. Let's see what we can do for this precious piece of creation."

As the audience strained to see the tiny ball of feathers in my hand, I turned to the a Capella group (we did use the odd instrument at times amongst our six voices). As we sang the opening harmonies to our first song - written to a bird - (!)

Crimson crested cousin of the cardinal
what say you
maybe we should pardon all
those crazy trash dumping huminals...[iv]

…the little bird struggled to its feet, climbed from the palm of my hand to my finger and began singing into my microphone. It proceeded to sing and chirp and carry on like a pro for the entire concert. Whatever had ailed it was being thoroughly cured by song. At one point, I tried to hand said bird to someone so that I could play the lyre and it walked quite determinedly up my arm, settled on my throat and flapped its wings throughout the lyre piece; after which it climbed back down to my hand and started singing into the microphone again.

The Kaahumanu centre has its stage sound wired to travel throughout the shopping mall; everywhere one could apparently hear several human voices combined with the sound of one very enthusiastic little bird singing with all its might. I remember only a little about the music of that concert, but the expressions on the faces of my fellow singers remain with me. And then there were the curious looks from those sitting in the audience, especially the notably huge Hawaiian or Samoan gentleman sitting up front. One has to know these guys to understand the surprise. They are pretty used to magic in their local culture; but amongst these crazy haoles (white people)?

At the end of the concert, bird still singing lustily, I began a quick farewell. "Look we didn't make this up, this little bird looked like it was dying and now look at it! This is a miracle!" As I said the word 'miracle' the bird gave one huge final call into the microphone and flew off through the open roof into the sky. Every head turned to follow its flight as it soared off to freedom.

I spent the next few days laughing....below is a long distance shot of that concert - the only one I have - from who knows which photographer. At the end of this tale I have expanded a detail - a little blurry but one can at least see the bird!

Once Upon an Earth Day part 2

There have been several other times when I have witnessed birds being almost instantaneously healed by song. Otherwise I might doubt that it was the song that did it.
Sometime around 1990 I was in a recording studio in Arizona. My musical-twin sister, the legendary singer Singh Kaur (1955-1998) and I were recording together. I do not remember what kind of bird it was that we found wounded and fading. But as soon as we began to sing, the bird rallied. We took it into the studio where Dean the engineer took out his video camera. Somewhere amongst the archives of 'Soundings of the Planet'

there probably remains footage of this particular bird clinging to the Neumann mike (one of the more expensive microphones around) singing gloriously into the mouthpiece. I am still not sure what instinct draws these birds to microphones. Born singers I guess. If I ever come back as a bird I bet you I'll cling to one too.

I was briefly teaching music at the local Waldorf School on Maui. It was May Day and, since Rudolf Steiner Schools like to celebrate seasons and festivals, I was sharing with the children in various classes some age appropriate myths and songs about the magic of Beltane. At some point in the day one of the kids brought a bird to me that looked almost dead; this one was also on its back, claws in the air and beak open. I found a wooden tray and placed some water with rescue remedy in it and a handful of seeds with the faint hope that during one of the classes, it might get well enough to eat. I remember talking with the kids about some memorable bird moments and then one of them suggested that they might sing something especially gentle for the bird. We decided upon an angel song that I had written and recently taught to them. As soon as those pure children's voices got going the sorry looking little bird stood up. The children all went wild with excitement and began making loudly excited kid noises. The bird immediately fell on its back and once again lay there with its beak agape. The kids hushed themselves in amazement and then proceeded to sing very beautifully, non-stop for the remaining 45 minutes of their class. We improvised a sign language to decide which songs to sing next. By the end of the class, the bird was pecking away at the

seeds and, it being the end of the school day, one of the children offered to take it home to her mother - a capable bird-lover. Some things you just can't teach out of a songbook...
I should mention my other favourite medicine for all things bright and beautiful. Rescue Remedy is one of Bach's flower remedies. It is made from the essence of 5 flowers; nothing that science at this point can measure. Purely vibrational it cannot therefore harm anything or anyone. It is generally preserved in dilute brandy so one needs to dilute it more before offering it to anything younger or more sensitive than the average bloke. But it has a curious power. It addresses shock. The more serious the issue, the more effective it is. I have seen it bring humans and animals out of coma and I have seen it soothe bruises of knee or spirit. Great for anxiety, stress, fear, panic etc., it is invaluable; I always keep a tiny dropper bottle of it with me. It saves lives and eases suffering. Drop it under a tongue, under a wing or on a heart. Remember to ask permission of others before using it on them. It is rather like prayer in a bottle. It always helps.

vi

5 ~ Aumakua

I saw an owl on the road
he landed time after time
and the look in his fearless eyes showed
that our lives are not defined
by our minds…

The Beloved and I fell instantaneously and incurably in love whilst dancing to the music of a Maui living legend. We rapidly became – and remain - inseparable. He being from the mid-west and more recently having abandoned various corporate career paths, probably didn't know quite what to make of my - ah shall we say unorthodox lifestyle? I was living amongst polyamorists and Ufologists (to paraphrase Voltaire, I may not agree with what you believe but I wholeheartedly support your right to believe it) in a jungle hideaway nestled amongst macadamia forests filled with squatting Hawaiian sovereignty claimants and several thoroughly dangerous outlaws. Around us flowed the streams and canal systems that provide much of civilised Maui with its water and above us loomed the virtually impassable peaks and ridges of West Maui mountains. To visit required traversing dirt roads and a causeway where several people had lost their lives in a flash flood only a season before. then one had to cross a small creek close to the house waterfall on a decidedly makeshift bridge made of one ancient and rickety log and then climbing a 30 foot wooden ladder and crawling through the pigeonhole that we affectionately called a door. Once inside it was delightfully snug with steeply sloping multi-angled ceilings and curious little windows that revealed glorious if tiny views of Maui's coastline across to the airport, down towards Ho'okipa and on to Hana from an angle never likely to be published in a tourist brochure. The house is now in the process of rapid decay that is the inevitable destiny of all wooden houses built amongst the jungles and forests of Hawaii unless their owners dedicate considerable portions of their children's inheritance towards maintenance that is so continuous and unforgiving that many eventually abandon it as futile. Besides which, the draconian zoning laws of Maui have clearly been designed to make all creative dwellings other than traditional grass huts and multi-million dollar property developments pretty much illegal. My erstwhile landlords briefly achieved local fame not to say notoriety by appearing on the front page of the Maui News as being the first folk ever to receive a one million dollar zoning fine; not, I must emphasize, for the questionable safety of my owl's nest, but for the gargantuan crime of having too many stoves on the property: Polynesian logic works best when it is sorted out whilst swinging on a hammock strung between two good coconut trees close to the shore with a sweet breeze blowing freely. Had Maui County Council buildings been designed with this fact in mind, many is the local law that would never have been passed by disgruntled politicians sweating in their business clothes and bored half to death in air-conditioned chambers where the true purpose of living in paradise is all too easily forgotten…but I digress! How dare I take a soapbox stand on local politics, while you, poor reader are waiting agog to understand the nature of the title to this chapter!

David was pretty unfazed by all these variables and despite his being an architect he held his peace regarding the various dangers posed to one's person or soul on any given trip to the house, apart from clearly stating his faith in and preference for monogamy at the outset. Having already recognised this to be a philosophical and practical choice for those who prefer peace over drama, and who desire to do something more with their lives than work out their relationship issues on a full-time basis, I was more than happy to comply and so he was becoming a regular visitor despite the obstacle course that lay between civilisation and his new love. His big yellow truck was equal to its part in the journey and his big full heart was similarly willing to undergo any number of tests and initiations to be near to me. I am a lucky woman…

And so it was that one dark and lovely star-filled night we were bouncing contentedly amongst the potholes and ridges that the locals ungrudgingly call a 'road' when suddenly out of the night swooped a large silent bird. It landed gracefully in front of the truck and in the glow of the headlights clearly revealed itself to be a pueo (the Hawaiian owl). Since I am accustomed to birds behaving in unusual ways only if they need help, I got out and carefully approached the owl who looked me squarely in the eyes and then very slowly spread its wings and flew up and off. I got back into the truck and we drove about 100 yards. At this point swirling wings almost brushed the windscreen as the owl landed on the road ahead. Again I got out to see if it wanted anything and again it stared into my eyes and then slowly unfurled its wings and flew about another hundred or so yards along the road before landing in front of us again; I got out; the bird looked into my eyes and flew slowly along only to swoop down again about another hundred yards on. This began to feel like a dance: humans, owl and big yellow truck. We remember that this happened at least five times. David was stunned, having never before experienced anything like it. I was a little more relaxed about it having spent measurable portions of my life amidst marvellous animal happenings – but nevertheless, I took careful note of the direction the owl took when it finally veered off and away from the path just before we reached the house driveway. It headed towards the city (as the owl flies) and on towards Haleakala, the better known of Maui's mountains.

As it happened I had a set of Hawaiian wisdom cards in my room with an owl on the cover; sure enough, the 'pueo' was described as an 'aumakua' – an ancestral guide in the form of an animal totem or a spirit messenger. The cards said that if the pueo appeared briefly it was a message from other worlds or dimensions but if it appeared repeatedly it was a warning. Both of us had been sufficiently affected by the magic of this animal visitation that we wasted little time in grabbing a few essentials and taking off in the golden chariot towards our new life together, where we eventually settled high on the slopes of Haleakala.

As it happened, in so doing we avoided a rather serious clash with someone for whom our new love was a threat to their sense of security. Departing in the middle of the night allowed everyone the space they needed to calm down and eventually harmony was restored.

In truth I shall never know what would have been the outcome had we simply stayed put that night, but somehow the synchronicity of the owl and the Hawaiian wisdom available to us seemed to flow like a river. I was guided away from my old life towards love and marriage even though as an artist I had avoided such a path for almost half a century. To ignore it would have been to swim against the tide. As it is, we remain happily married almost a decade on. And yet several continents and islands away from that first visitation, we still feel 'the owl within all owls' keeping an eye on us in ways too subtle to describe. This story has no end as yet. although the pueo did make a comeback as a postscript in the next story - about Australian parrots...

If there is more to this, I'll keep you posted…

6 ~ Parrot Tails

My mother Eve is an animal whisperer. She tells me she comes from a long line of Welsh witches on her mother's side; and that her father was known for rescuing sparrows which would then zoom around their kitchen all through the long English winters. For as long as I have known her, animals have been adopting her – wild, or domesticated, they all seem to trust her. There was the time when she took a young child to the zoo. A lion was pacing, restless in its unnatural enclosure. She spoke to it as she has spoken to every animal – straight from her gentle heart. The lion rolled onto its back and started purring. When a crowd of curious onlookers joined her the lion rose up growling and roaring at them.

It has always been like that with her...creatures just naturally respond to her.

It must be something in the genes. Her granddaughter, my niece, finally legitimized the passion by becoming a vet. I am grateful for this as we needed at least one in the family and I could never make the kinds of decisions vets have to make. Nevertheless, I have been party to some wonderful animal magic – quite the inheritance…Let's hear it for those native European ancestors!

But when our family emigrated from England to Australia in the early '60's, my mother had terrifying, if somewhat misinformed visions of man eating koalas and kangaroos roaming the streets of the far antipodes. They say we create reality according to our beliefs. Our ship arrived in Sydney Harbor around sunset. Some friends had organized a temporary rental for us in an old Federation style house in Mosman, not far across the famed bridge. By the time we arrived, it was dark. All night long the air was filled with howlings and roarings way beyond my mother's worst imagining. She hid her tears from us all and sleeplessly prayed to keep her precious progeny alive in this wilderness. The next day we found out that our house was situated just across from the zoo. We children spent many days of our first months in this new country sneaking between the bars of various animal enclosures so we could get in for free, unwittingly fulfilling my mother's worst fears for us all as we crept past the hyenas and water buffalos whose split level enclosures were far from the main entrance and the eyes of most of the staff. These seemed quite navigable to my brothers, so naturally I trustingly trotted along behind.

Eventually we moved (all our limbs still intact) to the Pittwater side of the northern beaches peninsula of Sydney. The previous owner of the little house which had been chosen entirely for its glorious view of bays and forests, asked my mother to 'take care of her birds' meaning the marvellous flocks of native birds that flourish there. And so for the better part of half a century, Eve's house was a haven for generations of Australian wildlife. It was completely pointless for us children to try telling her that humans are not encouraged to feed native creatures as from her point of view, the animals and birds were her friends and she would no more stop feeding them than she would stop feeding us and anyone who ever visited. My mother is a compulsive nurturer.

Hence by the time of the following story, each species had their own special dietary needs catered for; they had their own dining hours, water bowls, bathing dishes, crockery and dish cloths. The night creatures were carefully fed fruits and grains; I have watched possum babies on their very first venture out of the pouch, clinging to their mother's back, reaching out and taking a piece of pear from my mother's hand as if she were their own grandmother. The family gave up disapproval as it was just a waste of everybody's time. (What was the point? She and the animals seemed so happy together.) As Eve grew older and housebound, her shoppers would arrive with bags and bags of food never suspecting that almost none of it was for human consumption.

Parrot Tails Part 2

Time has made Eve frail. Eventually she had to let go of all the chopping and special feedings. The local wildlife appears to have effortlessly adjusted to the loss. There seem to be just as many birds and animals in the nearby trees and they all seem quite capable of foraging for themselves. For 45 years the bird woman of Salt Pan built bridges of trust between wild creatures and that most dangerous of all animals – the human. Knowing what we do now, I would not recommend that others follow her path, but love is a curious force with its own set of rules. Eve's love is famous amongst a special few – four footed, two footed, winged, furred or scaled.

She and my father were true beloveds. So when Harry passed away at the ripe old age of 95, I came over from Hawaii to stay with her for several months. This was shortly before she had to close down the 'soup kitchen'. It was a perfect time to write and one afternoon I was looking about for some inspiration.

I was sitting at a tiny little table with my laptop, when that supposedly quiet inner voice quite clearly said; "Quit looking at the keys" (I am that sort of typist) "and watch what is happening on the veranda. Just write what you see…" This is what unfolded before my eyes as I typed even more badly than usual…

"The parrots have me completely fascinated and evidently this one sitting on the veranda is quite interested in me. He has hopped along the wooden railing towards my room to watch me sitting inside what must appear to be an enormous nest; now he is resting. Apparently he is not able to fly. All the birds around here seem to recognize that my mother's home is a safe harbor. They just about knock on the door: local bird hospital.

This one literally tapped on my toenail with his beak as I went out yesterday afternoon. "Hello up there…ah I can't fly…um, can you help?" The trust from these birds is extraordinary. It overwhelms me. They are wild yet voluntarily tame and completely free. It is a joy unimaginable unless one has experienced it. Like the last bird we cared for, this little guy is gaining something from his apparent weakness. Vulnerability can open our eyes to new experiences. My eyes are unable to tear themselves away from this fellow who has conveniently decided to sit where we can see one another. Vulnerable as I am to many typos, I might learn something myself.

…I am essentially parrot based right now and since words have occupied so much of me since I could first comprehend them... parrot based is not a bad idea for a change; all feathers and simple stuff. After forty five years there is a legacy of trust between the birds and my mother. My voice is similar enough to hers I suppose; so I am being ancestrally included in the privilege.

Often I am stroked by a cloud of brilliantly coloured fluttering wings as I return home through the flock feeding outside her door. Some 35 or more of them will variously fly across and over me or stay put and just accept me as one of their safe humans. My cheeks will always remember the feeling of many parrot wings brushing softly against them.

Rainbow lorikeets tend to be pretty earthy for creatures with such incredible plumage. They are quite ruthless with one another; I saw two this morning roll this one on its back with their pecking once they discovered its food source. Mother then organized a shelter for him so he could eat in peace. He was recuperating at the far end of the veranda, feasting on fruit, taking leisurely hops to the water bowls (one for bathing one for drinking!) Then he climbed up the hose and rested against it for a long time, leaning against the tip with one leg tucked up - unusual behaviour for these lorikeets. We wonder - he eats and seems content to wander around the veranda but he has not flown since at least yesterday. Mum says they often do not survive once they come to her sick. So (naturally) I have sung to him and offered a spot of healing. He seems completely 'tame'- well, wild but trusting. Happy to hang out close up and eye to eye, he even considered climbing onto my hand (one claw over my wrist) then thought better of it. But now he is perched directly in front of me. We are definitely associating here quite openly appreciative, one species to another.

His back and wings are brilliant emerald green; a close inspection reveals that the underwing is dark grey with a touch of bright yellow. His head is virulent purple as is his mid to lower belly. His chest is vivid orange-red underscored with bright yellow and his beak is orange. His eyes are red circled with orange and are black or dark brown at centre. He and his clan are definitely not designed for camouflage unless they originated in a psychedelic world.

Flying flowers I originally thought but now I think flying jewels is more apt. Clowns of the bush is how most Australians know them. They are innately comical. It is rather like living amongst a cast of Disney characters. There was one we called Biki because of his twisted beak which crossed in such a way that it would not shut. Once Biki had laboriously chewed something, one of his tribe would snatch it from out of his uncloseable beak.

And so of course I started to feed him. Soon we were being watched. I remember the day before David and I were wed, the entire tribe sat on the rails watching while Biki waddled up to the veranda door. After we went away on our honeymoon Biki disappeared. I suspect fowl play.

Parrot Tails part 3

Recently a sulphur crested cockatoo required sanctuary for at least three weeks. He had an injured beak. At first I feared beak and feather disease as I was told that it is rampant amongst them. I called my niece at her veterinary clinic in Broken Hill. She said she thought it sounded like a trauma based issue and that his beak could grow back. Over several weeks it did seem to. We fed him mostly soft stuff like bread and he would sit munching on pieces of crust, holding them deftly like a sandwich clutched in his claw. He obviously enjoyed my songs, bopping back and forth as he ate and generally showing his appreciation as only birds can.

Cockatoos are much larger than lorikeets, remarkably intelligent and we developed quite a relationship. He brought his friends, to share in his good fortune. But these birds are known to be destructive if one isn't watching carefully. They can destroy wooden decks and window grouting. So mother insists on only feeding sick or injured cockatoos. It was extraordinarily easy to get this across to the flock using a combination of picture thinking, gesture and plain old words with plenty of emotional umph behind them. The tribe got it immediately and never again tried to eat with my wounded friend.

viii

But they did come to check me out. I was amazed at how the whole flock cared about their sick buddy. There were 'the girls' sitting up on a branch practically arm in arm – or would that be wing in wing? One of them was almost definitely his partner and she and her sisters would watch me closely as I fed him. Then came the tribal elder. He had sharply hunched 'shoulders' to his wings; one could have imagined rimless spectacles on his beak. He was clearly evaluating me as he stalked along the railing. I think of him as 'the Dean'. Then there was Prince Charming with plumage so blindingly white and sleek that he almost glowed like a unicorn. Impossibly handsome and with a marvellous sense of humour, he hid under the outer edge of the veranda floor, clinging on by his claws and then lifting himself up so that his face and beak appeared above the edge; when our eyes met he would duck down underneath again so that all I could see would be claw tips and an inch or two of his yellow crest. Any who have interacted with cockatoos know that I am not exaggerating. But I had never encountered the extraordinary variety of personalities present in a whole flock before. It was life changing to realize that so many unique characters are flying around in the trees, squawking uproariously as they soar across the bays and waterways. Eventually they seemed satisfied that I was an OK nurse and they left their friend to heal unsupervised. After several weeks of early evening feedings (just pre-sunset), my injured friend came one night and - like this little lorikeet has today - hopped down the veranda to find me in my room. I sensed it was to say goodbye. My mother fortunately took photos of us. He returned later towards dusk, looking me closely in the eye. At some point during this particular evening, another cockatoo - possibly his mate who had often hovered close as he fed and acted rather like a slightly miffed girlfriend, had flown down and taken his crust out of his claws. He had allowed this without the slightest resistance. Then he was gone. In stormy weather the cockatoos tend to go elsewhere. Mother and I returned from a lunch date several days later to find him on the tiny lawn along with several of his friends and his presumed mate. He was digging into the grass even though this involved falling rather ingloriously on his tummy. He did stop to say hi though. He waddled across the lawn to greet me at the car door, excitedly showing off his family of friends. This time he made it pretty clear (both Mum and I agreed on this) that he was healed enough to feed himself and that unless we would feed the flock - or at least his mate - he couldn't justify coming to us for dinner any more. He has not returned. But his time with us was complete. He had the softest features and gentlest ways that I have yet seen in a large bird. The first and last law of wild animal interaction is: "Freedom!" Non attachment is crucial. So many times I have laughed through tears as a creature disappears forever back into its true habitat.

So as I write a miracle occurs. This is quite what one might call synchronicity. I can hear the angels laughing – or is it the kookaburras? I am watching yon parrot and am drawn to go out and talk to him. He is sleepy, weak and sits with his back to me as I sing. After a few moments, he turns around on his perch on the rail and looks me in the eyes again. I notice his wing is slightly limp beside his back. He keeps his claw up under his wing and attempts to stretch but it hurts - he gapes his beak much as I would grimace if I were stretching a sore arm. So I get my homeopathic arnica pills (potency 30 C) and take a few out, asking his guardian angels (or whatever it is that assists birds) to help him to take them. I considered putting them in the water supply but since his drinking it would be a gamble, I thought I would try offering the pills directly to him first. He snapped lightly at me for putting something so very close. We had been closer before but I think he was in pain. Then, when I put down the tiny spherical pill, he looked at me rather quizzically and then bent over and picked it up in his beak. Being so round, it rolled out and fell off the wooden rail; we repeated this three times until I (hoping my human germs wouldn't harm him) bit a pill in two. He picked up the little piece and chewed it, staring at me while he did so. His eyes drooped closed immediately; the classic sleep of homeopathy (when one has chosen the right remedy). After a few minutes, he walked along the rail and stretched like a ballerina - his wing and his opposite leg - very yoga. Then he strolled back and ate the rest of the pill.

On mother's orders I was by this time feeding cheese to a magpie and a soldier bird. My friend joined us and ate cheese bits (unusual for a lorikeet – maybe he needed extra protein) and then he became quite energetic, hopping about with new energy. He avoided two other lorikeets that joined him as he fed from a bowl of grain I was holding. He looked as though he was attempting to get up on the rail again so I offered to assist. He refused my help and strolled to the end of the veranda. Then about 15 to 20 minutes after taking the arnica pill, he flew - rather unsteadily - down into the trees near the park. He had been 18 hours or more flightless at the bird hospital.

My day is made; my mother is in awe (at the parrot eating the pill as much as at the power of homeopathy). Then, just to add an absurd postscript to all this: I have needed a suitcase for my return journey to Hawaii. I went up to get the mail and it being council collection day, lots of discarded stuff is being left out on the roads and there was an old but solid Samsonite case. The thing is, it is perfectly parrot green. I am a barefoot healer and rarely get paid for my humble efforts; so this is quite an honour!

So some of you reading this might ask "What do you mean by: the bird 'refused' your offer of help?"

Well as I mentioned at the beginning of this story, I have been a wordsmith since infancy. And yet it has always been this way with animals. If one is willing to listen with one's senses and heart, animals communicate incredibly clearly. Horse whisperers, elephant whisperers, all people who spend respectful time with any kind of creature will often find that one forgets the verbal realm and finds oneself in a wonderland of body language, expressive tails, beaks, eyes, head angles and plain ole telepathy. Thinking in pictures is a major key. Our own minds seem quick to translate the images in to verbal thought.

Parrot Tails part 4

Some months later I read and grieve from a permanently altered heart. There is another chapter in the cockatoo tale. Our sulphur-crested friend returned the worse for his wanderings, his beak painfully re-injured; more damaged than before.

This time he could only eat soft things… He was with us for weeks. His trust and his sweetness were achingly pure as he weakened and occasionally seemed to strengthen. After a while, he could not fly with his flock. It was heartbreaking to see him straining his vision to follow their flight as he remained behind, high in a gum tree. But love - the animal human connection - was awesome to my soul. He began to fly from his perch only when I called that it was safe for him to come down. Other birds vied so furiously for his food that I had to become a protective warrioress on his behalf and on theirs. I suspected by now that this might be the dreaded beak and feather disease after all. I had extraordinarily vigorous arguments with a pair of lorikeets who perpetually inhabit the back veranda. They would flutter in the air in front of my face arguing in outrage while I tried unsuccessfully to explain that I was trying to protect their health. Then, having failed to convince me of their inalienable right to all food served at the soup kitchen, they would turn in mid-air and start punching one another in frustration over this impossible human; a flurry of furious wings. At times I would laugh for days after such encounters and at others I was almost totally exhausted as my own health was being challenged considerably at the time. I had to battle daily to keep the cockatoo food and water separate from the other birds.

I knew my mother could never keep this up. So the day before my plane departed back to Hawaii, I placed a basket on the veranda. I told the cockatoo that I was leaving. Not returning. We stared into one another's eyes. I saw he was very sick and weakening. He showed a kind of exhausted resignation and I saw too much pain.

I had called WILDS – the animal preservation folk - and Luci, my niece the vet. All recommended capture and a vet to check if he had beak and feather disease…if so, euthanasia. The disease is contagious amongst all parrot species.

I went to my bird friend and asked him if I could take him. He turned his back and faced away but he seemed to be offering his body to me (he could fly). I placed a towel around him. He

squawked and I let him go. But by then I felt certain. He once
again turned so his back was to me and presented his body to
me. This time I was more assured. Gentle firm strength; I placed
him in the basket.

Only my mother could have known how hard this was for me.
She insisted on driving with us – the vet was close. I sang to our
bird friend in the clinic and the vet was kind. I gave the bird
rescue remedy. But he was caged. I last saw him clinging to cold
metal bars, wings outstretched; eyes wild. Torn between two
evils, I was betraying my friend to save his flock.

The next afternoon I left to return to Hawaii. As the airport
shuttle bus drove from my mother's house, one white cockatoo
soared alongside us at the bayside edges…for more than a mile
it tracked our path.

I called from the airport and my mother told me the vet had
called. Our friend had a tongue infection and could not eat. Beak
and feather disease. He was gone.

Back on Maui, as we drove from the airport up the old mountain
road home an owl flew in front of the car like a beacon form the
bird tribes. At the house, way up on the slopes of Haleakala,
another one flew right up almost eye to eye with me on the high
lanai (veranda).

The first week I was home we drove to Little Beach down the
back roads amongst the desert prickly pear. On the road a pile of
soft feathers. We stop. An owl. It is…. dead? I contain the body
in a box. We put the box carefully on the rocks near the car at
Makena, a beach on the desert side with wild lands all around.
Voice says 'Must close the box thoroughly'. So I tuck the

corners shut. On the beach (a ten minute climb away) a sudden ache…Was the owl truly dead? I must go back. A man we know is leaving. We walk together to the car. The box is on the ground. I reach down heart pounding. The bird has moved! A face peers up from inside the box. Blood smeared. Mongoose; eyes wild with bloodlust. My friend is horrified. A mongoose could have done terrible damage to my face if the box had not been closed. After a while we are sure the mongoose has vamoosed. The box is quiet. We open it. The owl is headless. I see that it is my chance to give the rites of passage to another member of the bird tribes. I carry it to a fork in a tree and place a coconut shell over the body. I pay my humble respects; as I could not for my cockatoo friend.

Some weeks pass. I am sitting alone one day high on the Haleakala mountainside. Dismiss my dreaming if you choose. The cockatoo tribe spirit enters my quiet soul and speaks to me of my interference with their ways of deathing. I completely empathize. I offer them my humble apologies, my future service and my love. I offer to assist or be guardian to those who may benefit. Yet when does a wild animal truly benefit from human interaction? Only when the wild is fully respected as equal to or elder to the civilized. My system of ethics remains in uncertainty. Perhaps it would have been kinder to have killed him with my own hands. But my heart did not have that kind of strength. I am humbled, as is so often the case when nature comes to meet my half civilised ways.

7 ~ Bee-attitudes

I have given away diamonds - more than once although I have
never actually bought one - and I have not missed them. Yet
never have I mourned the loss of a treasure so much as the day
that I cast the mummified body of a big golden bee encased in
its little enamel sarcophagus down into the deep mountain valley
below where I lived on Maui in the last months of living there.
Perhaps I should explain…

From the earliest days on that enchanted isle, bees entered
gently and persuasively into my personal myth. I remember
living on the jungle side where an old tub in the garden allowed
me the indescribable pleasure of bathing under starlight with the
sweet Maui rains or the intoxicating radiance of the full moon
shimmering into the bathwater. One night while I was thus
luxuriantly abandoned, a honey bee kamikazed straight into the

moon reflection in the steaming water. By the time I had scooped it out, it looked thoroughly dead. Feeling somewhat responsible for this loss of life, I held the tiny creature in my palm, singing what I hoped was a suitable requiem. After a few moments of singing, one furry little leg stretched straight up out of the damp ball of bee fluff and waved itself in the air in what appeared to be a valiant attempt at dancing to my song. Inspired by this seeming miracle I continued to sing and by the time I had finished my bath, I had become the temporary guardian of a rather bedraggled wet bee.

Carrying it back into the house, I rigged up a little basket, hanging it from the ceiling light as tropical ants are ruthless. By morning the bee was awake and presumably hungry. Fortunately it was not difficult to sort out its dietary preferences. I put a drop of unheated organic honey on my finger and offered it to the bee which quickly put out its little proboscis and started to eat with considerable gusto. Shortly after, it was whizzing around the room looking whole and hearty. It took some organization to show it the door but eventually it found its way out and back to its life of bee-ness. I felt momentarily relieved of my responsibilities towards apis mellifera. Except that during my next bath, the same thing happened. In fact it kept on occurring pretty much every time I bathed. I became quite adept at scooping bees out in time to prevent coma but after a few nights of this, I decided it was time to intervene. As the next bee sat rather dazed on my palm I began a song of warning. After all, I rationalized, these guys dance the whereabouts of good pollen, tasty nectar and blooming wildflowers to one another so if I sing to them about dangerous hot water ponds in the night, perhaps this little critter will dance this caution to its hive family. I learned long ago that animals think in pictures so singing in my best bee voice I pictured the life threatening nature of the starry waters in the garden. The bee stayed for my song and then flew off. Never again did a bee dive into my bath.

My journey amongst natural forces on the side of a volcano in the middle of the Pacific Ocean was a colourful one and several of the stories in this collection emerged from those adventures. Over the years, occasionally feeding injured or exhausted bees I began to think of them as the 'cats of the insect world' since they really seem to both receive affection and to spontaneously reciprocate; unlike most insects which, in my experience do not share anything remotely akin to the kind of emotional life that I as a human inhabit. Although I have only recently been actually petted by a bee, I was kissed on the mouth by a whole bunch of them in upstate New York whilst preparing to perform a rather organic rock operetta we had titled "Sex and Mud and Rock and Roll". The tech team was horrified and began desperately trying to swat them away from me until I assured then that the bees were my friends – possibly my fan base in New York...

Bee-attitudes part 2

Some years later I found myself living on a property close to Makena on the southern desert side of the island. The last estate before the La Perouse lava fields situated by a well-known snorkelling beach and surrounded on three sides by the waters of a fish sanctuary. In this earthly paradise, I was home schooling two young German children and living with the family. I had my own little sanctuary amongst the shady foliage and early mornings I would walk amongst the phenomenal rock formations of the last lave flows of Maui which are only about 200 years old and are filled with marvels that only become apparent when one has the time to explore thoroughly. One morning, crouched down to appreciate a tiny oasis of life sprouting amongst the sharp black crags, I found an enormous golden bee struggling over the rocks.

ix

After watching for some time in wonder at its beauty, it became apparent that this bee-autiful bee-ing could not fly. I respectfully offered my hand and it unhesitatingly crawled onto my palm. Lifting it slowly to eye height I found myself gazing into the most startlingly glorious emerald eyes. Huge green eyes in a big furry golden body! If the ordinary bee is a cat, this one was a lion. In awe I invited this magnificent creature home for some r & r.

Another basket hung from yet another ceiling. Some more organic honey and if I remember rightly, bee pollen which I hoped would add some super-food strength to my fabulous new friend. This one was definitely a music lover. I would sit outside amongst the lush foliage and play my guitar; the bee would settle on the resonating wood and literally dance to the music. It was not the only insect to do so, but that is yet another story. For three days I was completely enchanted by this marvel and then almost biblically, on the third day, it slowly stretched its wings and took a first unsteady flight. Exhausted, it came back to me (I kid thee not!), ate some more honey and then flew happily off back to wherever it came from. Delighted, I continued my idyllic life. By the jewel like waters, I played the part of a tropical Mary Poppins teaching children in my chosen way which involved countless paintings, many songs composed on the spot, hundreds of big picture library books from which we effortlessly learned English, and extraordinary journeys into nature. These last were almost unavoidable as we were surrounded on all sides by some of the most magnificent wilderness I have ever been privileged to merge with. I watched as two little city kids born in a Berlin penthouse transformed into a pair of nature (and Hollywood) loving mystics – but that tale would involve a whole book.

About three months passed and once again I was sitting outside my sanctuary in the thick verdant shade when a big golden bee flew over, circled around me a few times then landed in the palm of my hand. It sat there for about an hour and then very gracefully curled up and died. I find tears rising as I tell you – the kind that recognise the miracle of existence. After a ceremony attended by, of course, the children and various other lovers of natural mystery, I laid the glorious golden form into a little enamel box lined with a cotton ball. I covered it with another piece of cotton and closed the lid. The box became a part of my tiny collection of very special treasures. Occasionally I would open it and there was the bee body perfectly preserved – it never rotted! Years went by and somewhere along the line some blue waxy plastic seemed to accidentally melt itself around the container. I tucked it into my treasure bag and there it stayed untouched for some 12 years. this story goes on, but since the next chapter involves an apparently domesticated cat, I shall place it in the endnotes at the back of the book.[x]

Bee-attitudes Part 3
having touched on the wonders of the personal bee, I invite you now to consider some very important information about bees. Firstly there is nothing about this creature that is not in some way beneficial to all that surrounds it. In some systems of natural medicine, bee venom is injected subcutaneously to

remove stagnancy and is known to help reduce the inflammation of certain types of arthritis. I have found that on the rare occasion that I have been stung, it has generally proved to be beneficial. It is as though that these creatures, having recognised me as an ally have proved to be quite accurate little acupuncturists. For those of you who are allergic to bee stings, I recommend carrying a phial of homeopathic apis 30C at all times. If you get stung, place 3-5 pillules under your tongue and repeat whenever the pain or swelling increases. For the rest of us, I invite us to consider this insect to be a globally significant ally. What bees do for our planet and our food source is phenomenal. I highly recommend Rudolf Steiner's lectures on bees and, more easy to read and equally wonderful, the beautiful book 'Global Hive' by Horst Kornberger, both of which address colony collapse from a completely fascinating perspective. Although I quote and paraphrase from both books below, I cannot recommend highly enough that you read at least Kornberger's book in its entirety if you have any interest at all in the survival of the biosphere within which we humans coexist with all other living creatures.

Rudolf Steiner gave his lectures in the early 1920's and although I have been a student of his work since my teens, it is only in these lectures that I have seen him address sexuality. Actually he defines the bees' sexuality as 'love life', delineating it from the sexuality of other similar insects such as the ant or the wasp. He says that the entire hive pours its love life into the queen, which Kornberger later describes as the reproductive system of the living organism that is the hive itself. Steiner goes on to say that this potentizes the quality of love in the hive and that the hive itself runs on love. The honey thus produced is a 'distillation'; the living essence of the environment is transformed by the love within the hive into sacred nectar. Kornberger states that no human being has ever yet witnessed the mating dance of the queen bee. But Steiner, whose ability to see more than most was the foundation of his spiritual science, says that the queen bee rises towards the sun; that only in clear skies does she ever mate, She then returns to her hive with enough seed to breed for at least a year, imparting the passion of her mating ritual, along with the wisdom and knowledge of the surrounding hives given by each of the drones who sacrifices his life for the next generation of bees.

Steiner, in 1923 went on the say that the artificial insemination of the queen bees that had begun some 15 years earlier, would, within 100 years, lead to the breakdown of the hive. The beekeeper with whom he was giving the lectures argued with him on this point, as artificial insemination was undoubtedly increasing honey production and the economic wealth of bee-keepers. Steiner simply responded: 'We can only have this conversation in 100 years' time'. In short, Rudolf Steiner predicted colony collapse disorder; neither as a result of pesticides, EMF's nor of the infestation of the Varroa Destructor mite, which although it is indeed wreaking havoc, has lived synergistically with bees since before historical records began. The original and underlying issue is the sexual demoralization of the queen. This has systematically weakened the love nest that was the pristine hive, thus allowing the numerous challenges in the current environment to overwhelm bee colonies worldwide. Kornberger describes this industrial rape: 'To witness the plight of the queen bee in this violent intrusive, mechanical procedure, her long slim body anesthetised and held in the vice of technological contraptions…a metal syringe injected into her abdomen… might provide the shock that we need. Compare this cold, clinical procedure with the ecstatic mating flight of a virgin queen; her foray into the open to mate with dozens of drones in mid-air, high-flying suitors from many local hives, each carrying the strength and expertise of their origins imprinted in their genetic material. Compare clinical insemination by way of syringe with this yearly ritual of drones giving their lives for the future of bees." In this man made interference pattern, the queen bee is killed each year and a new, genetically strange queen is forced upon the hive where since time immemorial, each queen has lived for about five years, swarming each year with a part of her hive to start a new hive, leaving her established hives in an act of evolutionary generosity, to the next queen who is incubating as she swarms. It is true that the queen bee is a jealous monarch. There is only ever one queen, and yet the entire life cycle of the hive is a continuous act of selfless service to that which Kornberger sagely describes as 'the Bee in all bees'. As he suggests, the natural hive is a perfect living example of collaboration over competition as a lasting evolutionary affect in natural systems. It was for many years a mystery to me that the more I devoted myself to the welfare of the biosphere, the more my nose was rubbed in the mess we have made of our sexuality as a species in virtually every existing culture on the planet. To now find that the demon behind colony collapse disorder was not only predicted by one of my most respected mentors some 90 years before its occurrence but that once again sexual abuse lies at the heart of the matter is something I am still absorbing as I write. In all my endeavours in the past quarter of a century – musical, theatrical, educational, psychological or literary, I have repeatedly found myself producing works related to the environment side by side with issues of sexuality. Sex and the environment weave together like coiled snakes or like the strands of our DNA. There is a code suggested in this that will not be denied. I invite you to take this to heart and to explore with an open mind, your own relationship to both.

The artificial insemination and interference with the natural genetic heritage of the bee was historically the first act of genetic modification. We are now witnessing the long term result in one crucial species. Einstein told us that the extinction of the bee would lead to the extinction of our own species. The collapse of the hive gives us a holographic representation of the long term results of sexual repression and abuse, the genetic modification of living beings and the over exploitation of a living eco-system where short term profits outweigh long term viability.

As she hovers on the brink of annihilation, is our furry-insect friend offering us one last service before she departs?

In her sacrificial dance she may be delivering us one of the most the most important messages of our time.

xi

8 ~ Arach-needs

Of the creatures greater and smaller that are described herein, the spider is possibly the least popular, given that I have yet to decide whether the snake moments merit a chapter…snakes are fascinating but have we had actual communion? Oh maybe once. Snakes are an aloof lot as far as I can tell. Perhaps it is because they have been given such a bad rap mythologically. Spiders however…spiders have woven their intricate webs into my own in ways that probably deserve title page honours. But who would want to read the book when so many humans are scared of them?

I ought to be. When my family moved from England to Australia in the early 1960's, my mother chose a truly glorious view in an area where few other than eccentric immigrants chose to make permanent homes. That the view came with a 'little shoebox' of a house was of secondary significance. The view some 50 years on is pretty much as it always was except that now there are hundreds of yachts moored where once there was only a handful, and the hillsides are filled with the sprawling cantilevered homes of some of the wealthiest Sydneysiders. The family home remains its humble little self. Who would know that amongst the sandstone foundations there once dwelt a daunting colony of funnel-webs, the female of which is possibly the deadliest spider on earth? Should I terrify you with some of the moments we shared with them? Or perhaps I should simply take a photo of the specimen which remains pickled in alcohol in a large jar on top of the old oak dresser. After 45 years it still looks distressingly powerful.

xii

A family friend attempted to prod at one with a pencil once and it snapped the pencil in half. They have a habit of hiding under and in things. One jumped onto my lap once while I was unearthing some old music manuscripts under the house. But my sister outlaw is the only person I have ever known to have been bitten and that was in her garden some miles from the ancestral shoebox. She being a level headed being managed to call emergency and survived relatively unscathed. She maintains that the spider did not fully penetrate her skin for which we are all lastingly grateful.

In spite of the real life Monsters-Living-Under-Our-House or perhaps because of them, I have since found all other spiders to be relatively benign. I am actually rather fond of them. In the subtropical rainforests of Australia I lived with some so huge and plentiful that few northern hemisphere folk would be able to sleep under the same roof with them. I learned (as all rainforest dwellers do) to be quite adept at either removing them or simply co-existing. It has never been an option for me to kill them. It was only when I grew familiar with the Native American creation myths and the powerful figure of Spider Woman (no, not the comic strip character, but maybe her ancestor) that it all started to fall into place. And then there is Maya, the mysterious weaver of the web of illusion in the Vedic scriptures of ancient India. But these mythical beings I encountered only after the events that I am about to share with you took place.

Arach-needs part 2 – Reweaving Old Paradigms

I have mentioned that there were many years of my life when I lived what one might call 'archetypally'. Archetype refers to 'the original model' and I was definitely concerned with origins.

Seeking for lasting solutions to the socio-ecological crunch that I could see was coming, I encountered many mythical aspects of the human unconscious, frequently ones that I had never personally heard of. This is an uncomfortable mode for a human but one I unwittingly chose by devoting myself to the service of 'Gaia' and then abandoning civilization for several seasons in order to know her better. For me, Gaia is a name that represents not only the living entity that is the biosphere of our earth, but a consciousness that includes the cellular memory of the evolutionary pathways that have been woven around this sphere and perhaps holds within it a microcosmic knowing of galactic and even universal consciousness. In this I know that my thinking differs from James Lovelock the founder of modern 'Gaia theory' as much as it does from the ancient Greeks. No matter; years of toe dipping into the realm of quantum mechanics and sub-atomic theory has altered forever my relationship to belief systems. They are blue prints upon which we create our reality and as we change them, our reality shifts accordingly. For better or for worse, this passionate linking of my consciousness with that of 'Gaia' yielded a magical lifestyle. Not an easy one, but definitely interesting. Picasso once said "One cannot be a magician all the time. How could one remain alive?" He is right. The demands upon the nervous systems of those who walk such paths are great. Some claim to do so. Some actually do. Mayan elders put it quite clearly to me once: shamans remain invisible. The public representatives, the ones who teach workshops and give private sessions to wealthy westerners are perhaps the lucky ones. They earn the respect of the so called 'world' and make a living. Shamans rarely do, being too busy living to spend time earning one and often they attract fear and derision for the odd lives they tend to live. I remember mentally designing a couple of bumper stickers once: "I can't afford to make a living" and: "I am not here to make a living; I am here to make a difference." I lived for almost 27 years on the islands and never did earn a taxable income. It was not that I did not work; it was that I worked on behalf of the natural world and nature supported me gently and magically. At times abundantly; at times I did not know where I was to sleep or what I was to eat, but always I slept amidst beauty and dignity and if I did not eat it was because I chose not to. I never begged for anything; all was given or shared freely as was my own energy. Integrity is the vital principle behind such a life. The magical way is open when heart and mind are coherent and part of that is always linked with the hearts and minds of others. At times I dwelt in temples and virtual palaces, clothed and housed as if in a fairy tale. As a guest or a house sitter to wealthy patrons, I would spend weeks at a time alone in a collection of large, delicately designed pyramids or in old half decaying tropical mansions on the ocean. In such places I would create music inspired by the long velvet nights with moonlit clouds scudding across windswept Hawaiian skies and wildly beautiful seas. Then I would depart with nowhere to go and maybe land in a tipi on the mountainside high above civilization. It was a glorious way to live and at times terrifying. For many years there was never security; just the fulfilment of living my dream; my music; my journey with Gaia. Wealth for a poet;

insane impoverishment for the consumer world upon whose farthest edges I dwelt; a Cassandra prophesying the unwelcome truth which is now hitting us all in the face.

Arach-needs part 3 - So what has all that got to do with spiders? Well it is by way of introduction...bear with me. Hawaiians call this 'talk story' so brew yourself a cup of tea and relax!

During these years I spent time as a musician amongst some of the most noted tantra teachers of the western world; we worked as a team towards freeing the long repressed female sexuality and towards finding the elusive balance between man and woman on a sexually dysfunctional planet. Over time I saw clearly how sexual harmony is critical to the health of the biosphere. This awareness has been brought home to me again and again over decades although it did take a long while to sink in. Hence I freely repeat this over and over to you, respected reader.

Are you enjoying your tea?

I was at the time, married to a man whose respect for what I represented as a voice singing on behalf of nature exceeded our personal relationship. After a while, we did not live together but he remained a staunch ally and offered shelter and food when I needed it. There were times when I was concerned that he gave to 'me' more than I was able to give to 'him'. But he consistently assured me that it was his destiny to serve 'the goddess'. He was often found with babies or toddlers hanging out with him while their exhausted single mothers took some time to themselves at the Duck Pond where he lived. This was a collection of little huts built in a valley close to a stream where several generations of ducks had happily found sanctuary. Abundant with luscious tropical foliage, bananas, guavas, avocados and papayas, there was often one or other little hut spare when I needed sanctuary. Frequently I would reciprocate by doing some much needed cleaning. Regularly I would find the dried out bodies of spiders dangling from ancient webs inside the dusty cupboards. I began to consider the metaphor. Female spiders are known for consuming their mates. I was concerned that this might be an aspect of our thoroughly unorthodox marriage. At both the personal and the meta level I wondered about feminine betrayal. We have made so much of men being the perpetrators in the sexual battle ground of the past several thousand years. Yet working in the tantra seminars I witnessed time and time again that women were practising subterfuge and blame and were often in denial of their own complicity in the warzones of their relationships. Victims and perpetrators play out a crazy tango worldwide. We will never be free until we are willing to take responsibility for everything in our lives. Easy to say, but it takes great courage and discipline to live responsibly.

Have you finished your tea? Another cup perhaps?

One morning having found yet another dangling spider corpse, I walked into the little kitchen pondering these issues. I noticed the flat white egg sac of a cane spider lying on the bench by the sink. Somewhat absently, I tucked it into a drawer but then I became aware that I was amidst the life cycles of various species of arachnid. The corpse in the closet was about the same size as the egg sac I had just found. After breakfast I went into the garden with my guitar and found myself on the grass watching two spiders – one was a 'happy face spider' thus called for the emoticon it has emblazoned on its yellow back; the other was some generic garden spider whose name I do not know. Side by side these two were weaving their webs across neighbouring rocks. I remembered hearing once that spiders, given minute doses of LSD (whose idea was that?!) are apt to weave wildly different webs and as I watched these two busily spinning it occurred to me that these creatures build their webs throughout the houses of humanity. Would it be possible to 'sing' masculine feminine balance and mutual respect into their weaving? A sort of homeopathy in consciousness? I grant you that unless one is an Australian Aboriginal this might sound like a long shot, but bear with me. I sang intent upon a new paradigm. The spiders kept on industriously weaving perfectly normal looking webs and I continued on with my day. Later I found myself on the grass rolling around clutching my womb. I had been learning to track my ovulation cycle as a part of feminine consciousness and I remember being fairly certain that I had indeed 'laid an egg'. A couple of ducks waddled by looking smug. It was true; I *was* making rather a big deal out of a very tiny egg…

That evening, I returned to the kitchen to find a large cane spider tearing around as though chased by a demon. She was climbing up and down all over the kitchen shelves and seemed absolutely frantic. "Oh!" I opened the drawer and offered her the egg sac. She stopped dead. Stretching out a long hairy arm, she grabbed the sac, tucked it under her belly and stalked off. As she left however, I saw something drop out of the egg sac from a tiny little silken thread. A baby spider so small as to be barely visible was left dangling from the kitchen drawer.

xiii

So which came first the spider or the egg?
Nothing in our world has yet suggested to me that spiders have rewoven the man/woman paradigm. Black widows still devour their mates and men and women still grapple with the age old battle of the sexes. But since that time I have been living in ever

85

increasingly loving and trusting relationships, culminating in a marriage of great harmony, creativity and ease. I guess I cannot save the world, but perhaps in trying, I am learning to save myself. Speaking of which…

Arach-needs part 4. Spider Protector

Look, you are probably going to find this pretty weird. So did everyone in the room with me when it happened. Fortunately there *were* several people; otherwise I might once again fear that I imagined it.

I had serendipitously befriended a unique New York psychotherapist (I seemed to collect them as friends, can't imagine *why!*) who hosted a radio program syndicated to 30 east coast rock stations where she answered teen questions about sexuality. Rambunctious questions to say the least. Taking some much needed R and R, she had been staying at the home of the two psychotherapists with whom I was living at the time. They were involved in a day-long intensive with her in their glorious jungle home. I needed to go through the living room where they were all working naked – well yes they were definitely not your average psychotherapists and this was the '80's in Hawaii in a very hot sunny room. A kind of post-Eden paradise, nakedness was natural around there. I figured that the best way to pass through unnoticed was to also take off my clothes and slip quietly by. No such luck. The New Yorker immediately noticed me and became fascinated. Soon we were off to my favourite mud and waterfall spot where for the first time she experienced the bliss of covering oneself in pure Hawaiian mountain mud on a warm day near a crystal fall. If you haven't yet tried it you should; spas these days charge a fortune for the experience although finding primal mud and pristine falls is less easy now than it was then. One thing led to another and within 24 hours she had invited me to sing at her Billboard keynote address in New York a couple of days hence, bringing jars of Maui mud so we could anoint the audience. Now I had just spent the better part of five years living either outdoors or very close to nature. Civilization was as big a challenge for me as wilderness is for the average city dweller. But the opportunity and the adventure were irresistible. 'Yes' it was and that evening we found ourselves at the tantra temple - also the home of a couple who taught internationally and with whom I was family. Everyone was relaxing in the large pyramid that constituted the main living area. I went to get something from a gift drawer under the pillared water bed in the sleeping pyramid and as I did I found myself asking for some protection on this journey into the belly of the beast so to speak. At that moment I opened the drawer and a happy face spider jumped out onto my arm and began to weave a web around me. I watched as it wove up and down and around my entire body for who knows how long; time, as is often the case when things get mysterious, stopped. Eventually even my eyelashes were cobwebbed. It was as if I was in a cocoon. Were I a fly I would have been toast. But being several hundred times larger than the spider I was simply amazed; as was everyone else in the room. At one point the spider drew up its forelegs as if to sink its fangs into me. A moment of fear! I instinctively shook it off and everyone in the room leapt back in a mutual gasp of horror as if we were all mesmerised. The spider climbed nonchalantly back onto my ankle and continued its work. At one point, another woman who was heading to the Amazon on a trek, grasped arms with me in a cross pattern. The spider walked up our arms and wove a kind of infinity web around us. The woman later confessed that, having a fear of spiders it took every scrap of discipline she had not to hurl the creature from her as it wove her in. Eventually, thoroughly cocooned, I went outside and the spider walked contentedly off into the night. I didn't need to think too hard about this; I was protected.

Staying in my friend's tiny penthouse apartment surrounded by enormous skyscrapers, I would dress down to virtual invisibility and walk 40 blocks to the gym late at night, returning after midnight because that was when the air was at its most breathable. One night, passing Central Park I found myself wondering: "am I taking this protection thing too far?" I looked down and there between my two wrists a spider had woven a loop of silk. Just as urban folk can develop a passion for the wild, I fell in love with NYC on those long late night rambles. Years later I wrote a rock opera based there. It opens around midnight of September 10th 2001 with this song:

THE STREETS OF NEW YORK

New York is filled with a soul like no other
each sister each brother
Belongs to a tribe that up close can look mean
But walk from your centre and feel yourself enter
the unique dimension where divine intervention
enters the New York scene

Consumer warriors prowling the canyons
catching the reek of the hungry and old
And up by the subway on Broadway a genius
squats down and outlines the mystery in gold

Feel the heart beat in the streets of New York
Dance with it, sing with it, breathe as you walk
You can invite Spirit in
Ah - for the streets of New York - that's a wonderful thing

Walking at midnight defying the dangers,
nodding at strangers and trusting their wealth
People have told me the Amazon's safer
And if I were mortal I'd fear for my health
So I walk from my centre and feel myself enter
the unique dimension where divine intervention
enters the New York scene

Ah feel the heart beat in the streets of New York
where no one interrupted my long late night walks
You can invite spirit in.
Ah the soul of New York is a marvellous thing.

9 ~ The Joyful Mystery School

The Big Island of Hawaii is unique. Its vast black lava fields, sharply forbidding to a casual eye, roll down to jagged cliffs, and black sand beaches, the instantaneous offspring of molten lava as it meets the ocean. Explosive elemental forces are the norm here. Tsunamis roll in from underwater volcanic activity; lava flows continuously for decades at a time, slowly consuming whatever lies in its path – newly laid highways, villages, ancestral homes, forests and the shoes of the overly adventurous. Mostly there is an odd gentleness to Pele's whims. Few are the deaths at her hand even though whole fields of lava are known to collapse into the sea and hikers are often left to make their own choices about what and where is safe to explore. Park rangers will close areas where they anticipate serious danger, but it is on this island that I have traversed the least safe natural places in my life; they were also the most awesome; not once have I regretted it; but then again, I am still here to tell the tale.

The Hawaiians have as many words for lava as the Eskimos have for snow. It is ever changing; in some places it has hardened into smooth, creamy swirls as if acres of cake batter were being mixed with an enormous spoon when it all got frozen by an ancient spell; then for miles it is indescribably harsh and ruthless underfoot; in other places the lava gets luminescent and glassy. Magnificent sculptures litter the landscape amidst rolling black waves, solidified by time but not very much of it. There is the sense everywhere that the land is not quite ready for human contact. I feel honoured to have walked on land that is still giving birth to itself.

Amidst the riot of lava and the rawness of it all, the Big Island exudes the brilliant vitality of youth. This brand new land breathes a wild exuberance: so many flowers scent the air; so much fruit falls luxuriantly from the rich volcanic soils. Where else in western civilization does one find papayas and pineapples 3 for $1 in the local markets? Still the island known as Hawaii holds mysteries and challenges. Volcanic gas, known as VOG and also as the breath of Pele, the volcano goddess, has high concentrations of sulphurs dioxide and trioxide; VOG generates acid rains that eat away at water pipes making the drinking water a challenge and it pretty much sends the local population to sleep by about 9 each night. VOG is a heavy lidded substitute for more generously oxygenated air.

Fortunately the soils are perfect for growing coffee and the Kona variety is highly prized worldwide. Locally it is an essential medicine because without it, little would ever get done. Maybe that this is where the term 'Polynesian paralysis' was born…

I'm comatose on the Kona coast
I'm comatose on the Kona coast
I drink Kona coffee to wake myself up
I drink kava to calm myself down
I'm a biochemical cocktail
Comatose in Kona Town!

Sometimes the breath of Pele swirls across the landscape for
months at a time, darkening the skies and sending people into a
kind of somnambulistic state of entrancement. The last extended
VOG cycle pretty much wiped out the farms in the far south of
the island; some were abandoned. But when the VOG cleared,
the soil was as rich as ever. There are herbal medicines that
make living with VOG easier and there are some folk whose
systems seem to have adjusted to the coiling, veiled atmosphere.
The Hawaiian Islands have a way of choosing their inhabitants.
Almost everyone is welcomed as a visitor. Only a few are able
to remain and thrive. It is wise to read the signs. VOG is the Big
Island's demarcation point. Handle it or leave.
Despite its challenges and perhaps because of them, the Big
Island remains in my heart as the most magical of islands; the
kind of magic that requires physical strength and discipline. One
gets to experience the mysteries by swimming, hiking and
enduring beyond the average human comfort zone. There is a
joy in this that only the intrepid understand.

The Joyful Mystery School part 2

It is here that generations of spinner dolphins have made a permanent home in their favourite bay, only leaving at times to tour the island coastline visiting the many whale species that live farther out in the glittering tropic seas or to welcome the humpbacks upon their annual return from the north. These dolphins have befriended the local human pod naming some with specific clicks and whistles; playing their leaf games and bubble games and enchanting the humans who are willing to observe basic cetacean etiquette. They are even willing to teach some of us clumsy two footed, quick breathing creatures how to dive and swim more effectively so we are better equipped to play with them. I first encountered the human side of this ocean family at a free form dance group that met twice a week in an old hall in the village of Captain Cook. I was struck by the sense of unity amongst the dancers. Everything was improvised, intuitive; my kind of dance world. But there was a cohesive quality amongst the dancers; more than I have found in other such groups. Many of the dancers swam daily with the dolphins. I joined both groups whenever I could, remaining always respectful of the dolphin rhythms. Sometimes the pod was keeping to itself - time to let them be. But at other times they were wonderfully playful. Many of the human swimmers told stories of their experiences with the dolphins that raised the hair on my arms and neck or drew tears from my heart. But others' stories are no longer accurate in my memory and so with respect, I can only tell you of what occurred first hand and hope that you will somehow hear more of these tales. The dolphin is a wonder. Some say that had it evolved with an opposable thumb, it could have ruled the world. It is my perception that dolphins are too wise for that and too light-hearted. Theirs is a wisdom that exceeds intellect, as any who spend enough time with them will tell you, unless of course the people call themselves 'scientists' and' trainers': the kind who remove the dolphins from their natural habitat and then fool themselves into believing that the tests imposed upon the captives are relevant. I once pointed out at a symposium on cetaceans that were I held against my will in a cage, I would most certainly do all I could to sabotage whatever information was being forcibly extracted from me. Dolphins are for the most part gentle and delightful, but they are quite capable of fierceness, jealousy and possessiveness; their emotional life appears to run a full spectrum of its own and may well include qualities we have yet to embody. I can only say that the more time I have spent amongst cetaceans the more respect I have for them. I have frequently felt certain that the creature with whom I am interacting is more conscious than I am in ways that are impossible for me to explain for the simple reason that they are operating outside of my own range of experience. I have felt this even more amongst the humpbacks than amongst the dolphins with whom I sense a gentle camaraderie. I have always interacted in their environment where they are far more powerful than I am. This is humbling in a healthy way. They have often been helpful, happy to educate me and clearly protective of my safety.

I remember one rather dark, voggy morning standing at the edge of the bay as a woman ahead of me prepared to dive over the intense waves that were back-crashing to and from the rocky shore. "There are sharks in the bay today' she said gaily.
"Then why are you about to swim for hundreds of yards out there?" I asked in disbelief.
"Oh the dolphins always take care of me." She replied nonchalantly, and dived in. (I didn't join her.)
One morning swimming in one of their favourite bays with my partner, I noticed a small white dolphin rather apart from the pod; being something of a loner myself, I felt attracted to her. She also noticed me and before long we were swimming together quite companionably. Many 'dolphin folk' try to explain what happens to one's brainwaves when swimming with dolphins but I have yet to understand it. All I can say is that it is an altered state devoutly to be wished. Time is measured (if at all) in how long one can remain underwater on one breath. I have never used scuba equipment – it feels too confining for me while the dolphins are so gloriously free – but I find snorkel, mask and fins are essential. On this particular morning I followed the little white dolphin's lead out into parts of the bay where I had never been before. At a certain point she turned with a little jump; she was clearly shocked at how far we had strayed from the pod – and perhaps safety. At that exact moment a great big dolphin glided up between us and guided us back. I was gently taken straight to my partner. I have never figured out how the dolphin knew we were connected. We were a very

independent pair and did not swim close or show much in the way of demonstrable 'coupleness' either in or out of the water. To say that dolphins are known for picking up on subtleties is to understate the issue. Apparently one researcher having spent three years developing tests to measure dolphin potential with numbers was able to prove that the bottlenose dolphins sorted out the mathematics within minutes and then went on to demonstrate their ability to measure the age, size and variable densities of the testing rods used, almost like carbon dating. Pods always know when a woman is pregnant – often before she does - and there are mothers to be who have made a point of swimming amongst dolphins throughout their pregnancies as they are given very special treatment. Others bring children with special needs – particularly autistic children – to swim amongst them. Having a background in Rudolf Steiner curative education, this makes sense to me. Autistic children have trouble with the ordinary human 'ego' – they are generally more comfortable around for example, children with Downs' syndrome who are more universal and whose individualities are less pronounced. The dolphins appear to have great empathy without being personal for the most part. I do not wish to place them on any kind of anthropomorphic pedestal – they would swim off immediately... The fact is that they experience reality in a different dimension than we land-dwellers do. Their brains, though comparable in size to that of humans, relative to their bodyweight, appear to have a different emphasis. Their limbic brain is predominant, suggesting that relationships are considerably more significant in dolphin society than in human.

Although I have been fascinated by cetaceans since childhood, I now believe that it is inappropriate to attempt to compare dolphin and human intelligence. Each is worthy of respect and each is unique.

The delights of human dolphin interactions in the wild do have some potentially serious consequences. We do not know much about immunological factors between species. It is also common that visitors get so excited by the dolphins that they fail to remember that in dolphin habitat we need to behave with respect and empathy. Dolphins do not sleep as we know it. They are conscious breathers. They go into a certain type of slow swimming, deep and quiet. This is not a time to intrude. And as with all human interactions with the wild, there comes a time when our very numbers damage the environment and interfere with the lifestyle of the creatures by whom we are so fascinated. Dolphins are known for their 'polymorphous perversity' meaning that they delight in unrestrained sexuality amongst generations, families etc. This has proved to be a successful means of sustaining their species for millions of years. I know of some extremely sensitive folk who have been permitted to swim amongst them during their frolicking, but one can imagine that boats full of gawking tourists might interrupt the flow of their mating rituals.

The Joyful Mystery School Part 3

I am always delighted by dolphin interactions out in the deep ocean where the dolphins come to me. These purely voluntary meetings are sheer delight. Always they have been associated with sound. Having trained with acolytes of Rudolf Steiner, a part of my consciousness is often exploring sound qualities and possibilities. The ocean presents certain challenges. As soon as one exhales enough to yield appreciable sound, one has to rise to the surface to breathe. Sounding through a snorkel often sounds absurd but creativity works within its limitations. One morning I was busy exploring what was possible with a snorkel when suddenly I found myself flanked on either side by a large dolphin. Each was looking sideways into one of my eyes and although I tried not to impose my take on the situation, I got the clear impression that along with curiosity, there was more than a gleam of humour in those sidelong glances. We streamed along together for a while, me making ridiculous noises as I sorted – or snorted out breath, snorkel and water.

This seemed to grant me an introduction into the pod, proving my theory that sometimes one has to be willing to make really weird sounds (i.e. make a complete fool of oneself) in order to explore what is possible. I had the sense that those playful creatures enjoyed having a human clown in their midst…

Getting back to the deep ocean… The first time I ever swam way beyond my own safe limits was in passionate and fruitless pursuit of a whale pod with whom I had been sharing some wild sound interactions from the southern shore of Maui (see Treestory). This was before the law banned humans from chasing whales (believe me, a human without a boat is not capable of chasing a whale). I was, however oblivious to either of these issues at the time. Off I went into the wet wilderness until I found myself in some kind of rip, too tired to swim any further. At the time I was living on the edge. I do not recommend anyone following my lead on this. The Hawaiian oceans are deceptive. Gloriously aquamarine to deep turquoise and often about 80 degrees F, they are nevertheless just as capricious and ferocious as. if more seductive than, the most grey/green northern or southern oceans. But there I was and fortunately rather than panic, I simply rested on my back for a while and started to explore a particular sound quality that one of my earlier teachers had presented which involved sounding though one's ears. I recall this brilliant Swiss gentleman at an Anthroposophical conference in Australia singing with an angelic expression on his face. The sound came not from his mouth; it seemed to be emanating like a halo from all around his head. I studied with him and yet I found this technique to be elusive. One directs the sound through the Eustachian tubes. In my experience this was an almost metaphysical skill just as the split tones and throat singing found in the Himalayas can seem to the uninitiated.

Anyway, floating there on my back, ears in the water, too tired to swim but pretty relaxed, I inadvertently managed to clear my Eustachian tubes. I noticed that the water was echoing with an unearthly sound which I gradually realised was coming from me. I found myself surrounded by a circle of dolphins leaping in a kind of ritualised dance. The leaps seemed to coincide with the high notes. In an altered state of yet another ilk my conscious mind tried grasping at something with which to recall the moment: "They look like the dolphins surrounding an ancient

Greek urn." I guess that made me the urn. Looking back at that fateful winter, I can certainly see that for one sacred season, it was given to me to play the part of a modern day Delphic Oracle. (See Treestory).

A human ally was watching from the shore and decided to swim out in case I needed help. I didn't. After the dolphins left, I had all the energy I needed to swim back. He told me later that the sound had reached the distant beach – not a volume of which I am normally capable - and he affirmed that the dolphins were leaping in response to the various pitches. Once again had there been no witness to this, I might have had trouble believing it actually happened. The internal dialogue had been subsumed by the mystery of life. Decades of meditation have seldom silenced it so; only immersed in nature, in the presence of death or in profound sexual ecstasy has my enculturated mind been completely stilled. Mothers tell me that they also experience this at birth.

The next time dolphins found me singing in the open ocean was very light-hearted. Once again off the Big Island, I was fooling around with sound when a pod swam up in a very playful mode. For over an hour they cavorted with the two of us, swimming us dizzy and filling us with joy. It is as though they weave a magic web amongst one's synapses and priorities shift. Many dolphin lovers try to describe it. It seems to remind us that the true purpose of life might well be happiness and that this is really quite a simple thing.

The only time I have witnessed negative emotions amongst dolphins has been when they are captive. Watching them in

tanks I have felt their deep sadness, neurosis and heart rending listlessness. I have learned that in general, these creatures who can live for at least 35 years in the wild, often live no more than two or three years in tanks. It was for this reason that I found myself once, armed with my lyre propped up against a lectern, singing to the Maui County Council. They were considering an application for a dolphinarium A storm of protest arose from all parts of the island culture.
So far Maui has managed to keep her dolphins free...

xiv

CATCH THE MIDNIGHT SKY [xv]

There once was a time when a human slave
was a matter for commerce or daily trade
then America fought the civil war
so the human race could walk free once more.

Now the dolphin has since ancient times
been honored for the sanctity of its mind.
Oracles, legends, mythology -
all attest to the mystery.

Who would even try to catch the midnight sky?
So please leave the dolphins in the seas.

The great white fathers acquired their wealth
Land theft genocide, slavery and stealth
The past is forgiven - forgotten by time
but the responsibility of now is mine.

Who would even try to catch the midnight sky?
So please leave the dolphins and the humans free

10 ~ Bird Mother

Only white men would build a three storey concrete block of apartments on the rocks virtually overhanging the wild Hawaiian ocean less than 100 miles from an erupting volcano. My partner's mother had Parkinson's; her dream was to live right by the sea and so we cared for her there in some of the last seasons of her gentle life. In heavy weather we were splashed on the upper storey lanai (veranda) where we slept; salt coated everything in the tiny one room apartment. On the ground floor below us was a restaurant. Palm trees lined the parking lot. Next to us Magic Sands Beach disappeared for about half of each year, returning overnight sometime each winter in a frenzy of raging, deadly surf. A feng shui nightmare, it was fascinating to live as an air breathing mammal above the absolute wilderness that is the truth of the ocean. I have spent several years living on ocean front properties in Hawaii, but even dwelling on a beach without shelter for eight months, I was not as close to that watery enigma as we were in that apartment. …

103

xvi

I returned from a gruelling three day training in sexual abuse crisis counselling on the other side of the island to find a tiny ball of scowling black fluff with a bright yellow beak, sitting in its nest which had apparently been found in the driveway to the parking lot below us. It looked like a miniature primate; none of us knew what kind of bird it was and therefore no one had so far fed it. All I knew about birds apart from singing to them was that they eat their weight in food every day. Being hollow boned, this doesn't add up to much, but fasting is not an option for any infant. Several calls to vets and various animal lovers finally yielded up some significant advice "It's probably a sparrow; they look that way when they are very young. If you feed it infant bird formula it might live; otherwise it will not."

It being Sunday evening, The Big Island was fast asleep. Infant bird formula was a dream. I liquefied some papaya and banana and fed the brightly beaked ball with an eye dropper, petrified that it might chomp on the glass and die. Life had thoughtfully provided it with its very own nest so we merely added a small box, something soft and a low wattage light to keep it warm. Somehow it survived its first night amongst humans. Early Monday morning found me hastily acquiring the accoutrements of bird mothering: a plastic dropper and infant bird formula with all its complex instructions. It was clear that this was a big commitment; feeding every hour, cleanliness, warmth and of course, love. The last part was easy. Infants of every species are evolutionarily designed to melt the hearts of all but their predators.

Now many a human has raised baby birds and animals. Some say that one hasn't lived until one has accomplished this. The fact is that many of these sensitive little critters die. It was only experiencing the devotion that is required to raise one minute little thing from half a little finger size to about a full little finger size, that I grasped the incredible care that nature lavishes on all of her children. Life is precious; especially to mothers who invest so much of their own life force into their young. Perhaps all warriors should be required to raise an infant single handed before they go off to war. They might be less inclined to kill. There is an art to bird feeding. It is important to keep feathers clean – partly because of insects (an ever present danger, especially in the tropics) and partly for skin health. It took a while to sort this out but by the end of our first day together, accompanied by some soft singing, we were pretty well connected; every time I came near, a wide open yellow beak emerged from the pile of blackish brown fluff; ah motherhood... Some more information came our way: "Do not try to release it too soon. Youthful orphans do not survive. Only if you keep it for the full duration of its growing (at least six weeks) will it have any chance out in the wild. Good luck." My partner and his mother were soon heading off to the mainland for the summer. It seemed that I was to stay put, bonded by the beak so to speak. Before they left there was one night when I had to be away. I asked Peggy if she would feed the baby. Parkinson's is not a happy disorder as it affects dopamine production. I saw that the little thing was touching her heart and thought it might be good for them both. That night, swinging in a hammock by a deserted beach I had a clear image of Grandma trying to feed said infant with shaky hands. Sure enough, when I returned, the little one was completely plastered from head to foot with yellow infant formula; the matching yellow beak and the look of such surprise in its eyes were too much for my diplomacy; I laughed until I cried. Fortunately Peggy also saw the joke. I remember sitting for over an hour in the sun, carefully melting concretised formula off fluffy down; the tiny bird shivering while I sang to it and tried to keep it from freezing to death. After that I rigged up a laundry basket with a baby's mosquito net over it, adding some twigs and bits of nature to give it some character. This became our papoose. Baby and I were a constant item. Shopping, dancing, sweat lodges, music festivals; wherever I went baby came too, its basket hanging safely in a shady tree. It quickly became the most delightfully happy little character, enchanting everyone who met it. I remember spending a few days on a wonderful wild ocean front property where we all slept outdoors. At some point three of us were hanging out under a large mosquito net with the bird. The little one came right up to my eye, peering most intently. One of my friends murmured some concern, beak being millimetres from eyeball, but trust had entered our relationship and I was not concerned. The little fellow (I think it was a 'he' but I will never know) carefully started to preen my eyelashes with his beak. I remember feeling this unique sensation and trying to imagine how enormous was my eye to him – about the size of his head.

Bird Mother part 2

At this point I have to explain: I never gave 'it' a name. I was trying unsuccessfully to prevent 'it' from becoming humanized or domesticated. In a one room apartment, buckled into car seats in a laundry basket and amidst all my cultural shenanigans, this was an absurdity, but I always kept a part of my mind clearly attuned to his (he really was never an 'it') eventual freedom. He was a being of great light with a personality as big as the moon but he was also a wild creature. There was not a single negative moment in our relationship and since I always cherished his eventual liberation, even maternal attachment was not an issue. He awakened me to new levels of joy, inspiration and delight that were out of all proportion to his actual size.

At times he would sit on the high shelf by the tiny bathroom window looking out to the palm trees where, I realised, lived his tribe. I assured him that soon he could go out there to join them but first he had to learn to fly. This began in the bathroom where we spent quite a bit of time, partly to save Peggy's apartment from bird droppings. The first flight of a bird is momentous, like the first steps of a baby. From my shoulder he would sit and puff and puff as though to gather strength or courage and then, madly flapping his wings he would aim for the little window. The first several times he didn't make it and would slide down the wall to the floor, flapping furiously and scrabbling with his claws, desperately trying to maintain altitude. Once back on my shoulder, he would fall asleep exhausted for a few minutes then wake up, eat a little and try again. Perseverance furthers and inevitably he learned the art. He flew delightedly around the little apartment and found special spots high up in corners where he could sleep independently and begin to feel like a real bird. By this time, his fluff had made way for feathers, revealing him to be the most ordinary looking little sparrow that I have ever seen. He was distinguishable only by one errant feather which would always stick up on his head. I had reason to be grateful for that feather later on. Thinking back, had I ever named him, it might have been 'cow-lick' but fortunately something stopped me.

We loved one another without reserve, and were in constant communication. He chirped and chattered and he loved it when I sang. He would sit on the microphone with his back to me and fluff out all his feathers as though to absorb the sounds as they poured through him. It was an honour to have such a viscerally enthused audience, as I was, at the time, planning to record a new album of songs. I have over the years hocked heirlooms, jewels, anything short of my actual soul to record, as being an unknown independent, few funds were ever available. Lack of money has often slowed me down, but so far it has never stopped me. This time, after a year of voluntary service, all I had was the inspiration of my heart. A relationship of ten years although amicable was definitely ending and I felt that to record a CD would also be excellent therapy. I sat quietly, alone in the apartment where I was welcome to stay over the summer if I so chose, attuning myself to the task at hand; finding the courage and the determination required to fulfil yet another part of my life's dream. As is my habit in such moments of transition, I consulted various oracles, the I Ching etc. attempting (usually unsuccessfully) to choose the songs to add to a new CD. I would then play these to myself and by default to my bird friend. Of all the songs I played, there was one to which he responded in ways that left all the oracles for dead. Wherever he was perched, once I began this particular song, he would zoom down to me and get wildly excited. I wish someone had captured him on film. He was thoroughly Disneyesque at times; no one ever communicated to me more clearly than he did about pretty much everything that mattered to him. And this song really mattered. He even once (literally!) grabbed the volume button of my keyboard and started hauling on it as if it was a worm he was trying to pull out of the ground – or was he trying to turn up the keyboard? His enthusiasm for life was in all ways boundless but for this song it was phenomenal. I had written it some years earlier on a touring visit to Australia. A woman I had known decades earlier had experienced considerable tragedy in her life and for her birthday I had dashed off a 'poem' and tucked it into a card, leaving the original to disappear under the couch where it was discovered by my travelling companions. "You've written a new song!" they said. "No I haven't." 'Yes, we found it while we were vacuuming!" And so I added music. The song then remained quietly underground until the bird's excitement brought it out of hiding. I had not seen Carol in years so I also dedicated the song to a family whose first baby was about to be born. This was one of the blessed children whose mother had swum daily amongst the dolphins during her pregnancy. The week that the CD was released some months later, I received 2 emails back to back in my inbox, one telling me that Carol had died peacefully that day. The other told me of the birth that same day of the baby boy who was, no doubt, born to turn the tide.

BORN TO TURN THE TIDE

Slow sometimes the journey
from birth to death to birth again
There's no rush though
from breath to breath -
to Earth and then to Heaven
Somewhere deep inside
beyond where the demons hide
beyond the agony
beyond the bliss
beyond the ecstasy of a last kiss
Does humanity have to endure all of this?

There's some who say it's worth it all
as humans rise and angels fall
Beneath the skies, oceans parting
love is betrayed and vows are broken
Behind your eyes
gods are laughing
worlds are made and hearts are open
And somewhere slowly
deep inside
a love is born
a love is born
born to turn the tide

Bird Mother part 3

In the meantime, one somewhat culturally sophisticated little
sparrow was growing up. He was gradually showing his ability
to handle the foods of adulthood – scattered seeds etc. - so I
rigged up a large four poster mosquito net over the French doors
providing him with space on the outside veranda as well as
inside in which to develop his muscles and expand his view of
reality. He was zooming around like a pro by now, completely
in love with life. The time was approaching when he needed to
become a free bird and I started to whisper to him of the world
amongst the treetops with all the other birds and creatures he
would encounter out there. I assured him that if he chose to
remain with me, I would always love him but that I was going to
be 'migrating' soon to another island and probably he would be
happiest amongst his own kind. He listened to me as solemnly
as such a little joy beam possibly could.

July the 4th seemed to be an appropriate day to lift the net and
show him his freedom. He whizzed out towards the vast ocean
and taking in the enormity of it all, he did a complete double
take in mid-air. He flew back to my shoulder trembling and
nuzzling my neck for all he was worth. Realising that the sight
of the enormous ocean was probably not in his best interests, I
walked with him down the stairs and out towards the beach
showing him where he had been found in his nest and pointing
out to him all the other birds flying around. He flew off. I stood
for a while, breathing deeply and then turned towards the
apartment. Before I made it up the outside stairs, he was back

again, exhausted on my shoulder. We went home together for dinner and an early night. The next day we tried again and he flew off down the line of apartments, apparently dropping in on at least one couple who told me some time later that they were amazed to find a sparrow chirping merrily on the man's chest as he was awakening in his bed.

At this point I thought he was surely gone, since he did not return for over an hour. I went off to do some shopping. As I pulled back into the parking lot, a little lightning bolt appeared out of the blue. He was fluttering in front of my eyes, chattering with immense excitement telling me about all his Adventures, whereupon he once again dropped onto my shoulder and fell asleep. By now we were acquiring some notoriety amongst the other apartment dwellers, as local sparrows were not known for this type of behaviour.

On the third day, a new look came over him – a certain seriousness. I sensed that he was saying goodbye. He was ready to make his way amongst his own kind. I felt a kind of exquisite pain as he flew off (now I know where we got the phrase 'leaving the nest'). That evening an intense tropical storm hit. Kona storms are known for their ferocity throughout the islands. At dusk I stood sheltered on the outdoor corridor watching as hundreds of sparrows lined up to tuck themselves between the waving palm fronds which were at eye level to where I stood. When it comes to food and territory all birds are pretty fierce and I watched for a seeming eternity wondering how my little orphan could possibly find safety as the new kid on the block. In the next few days I learned more about sparrows than I would have thought possible. It is interesting how little we see until we are motivated to really look. I have viewed these common little birds in a new light ever since. Could each of them have souls as extraordinary as that of my ordinary little friend?

A few days later I went upcountry to Waimea to housesit for a few weeks where it was possible to do my own recording far from the sounds of the ocean and the equipment-crippling salt spray. After three weeks I returned to Kona amidst a heavy spell of VOG and I knew that my body could no longer tolerate that mind-numbing atmosphere. I packed my few belongings into my car and booked it onto the boat to Maui. The morning that I was to fly, I awoke on the veranda to find a little sparrow sitting on the end of my bed watching me with a familiar look of solemnity and love. I recognised him by his cowlick.

My friend had come - perhaps to bid me farewell.

xvii

11 ~ Close Encounters of the Fish Kind

A typical 'Maui Family' whale watch cruise generally involves a catamaran full of free spirits: captain, crew and merry Mauiians; clothing optional, singing, dancing, playing, praying and sharing food, affection and joy. Many cruises and plentiful tender celebrations over many years have made for a sweet filial intimacy amongst folk of many colours, generations and beliefs. Some bring instruments. Whales love music.

This will be a ride into whale territory near to the end of the season. The humpbacks are starting to leave for their long journey north.

We stop sailing at some point to swim and sing and be in the deep blue. There is a hydrophone connected to a speaker so we can listen to the humpbacks from above. Their song is different to any I have heard before. But then it's always like that. Songs change each year. This time I hear massive layers and range. Almost a cacophony; like a meeting of strong wills all saying their piece and not necessarily agreeing.

I listen, ear to the tiny speaker and at first it seems as if I will cave in with fear at an ecological level; grief so deep.[xviii] Then I tell my heart to be quiet and quit projecting my own stuff onto other life forms.

Once I dive beneath my own chasm of whale worry, I start to sense a more majestic appreciation of time. This is definitely coming from beneath me. Vast cycles of ecological change and shift. Huge time spans. The record keepers some call them. I am beginning to appreciate what that might mean. Thirty million years is a long time to be a successful species roaming the planet oceans. Makes us humans look like infants.

My intuition is to listen uninterruptedly from above. Until at some point I just have to dive in and hear with my own ears. There is a child standing on the step hesitant about getting into such deep water. I move her mask from the narrow space at the back of the boat and slide in. I make note of the drift of the ship and turn to take a deep dive down…

…straight towards a large silver creature rapidly approaching me from way down in the incredible jewel blue, blue blueness that is Hawaii beneath the surface. Our eyes meet. I can only see its head and its tail; its trajectory is directly angled towards me. I assume it's a dolphin. Foreshortened, I cannot see its length. Its mouth opens twice, not wide. Those are not the teeth of a dolphin.

Some part of me notes that its eyes as we stare at one another look more curious than predatory. It does not have 'a lean and hungry look' but my first conscious thought is to get everyone in the water back into the boat. Later I am grateful for this; we get to know ourselves in such moments. As I glide over the step in my wetsuit and fins, for once moving fast in that gear that feels so impossibly awkward on land, I call as tonefully as I can, "Shark!" I note that the child on the step has listened to her guardian angel and has hesitated long enough to remain safe. Everyone comes aboard and the captain – quite at home in that vast blue – jumps in to check it out…he is relaxed as he emerges. The guys who captain ships in Hawaiian waters know things about the sea they sail on. They have to. And this man seems to know more than most. "Big fish," he said. "Probably safe. Swim at your own risk." He was grinning.

Right, I thought. Big fish. It is probably bigger than me and that is plenty of shark. It gets the ocean, I'll take the land. It's a reef shark apparently. Not dangerous to an adult…

Several intrepid folk get back in – close to the boat. I consider it, admiring their courage. Jump back on the horse again.

But then they didn't dive straight towards that oncoming mouth rising from the deep did they? And besides, newly married. I don't think David would approve of my risking his wife.

PS I was delighted that I wasn't afraid but I noticed later that my knees were a little shaky. I listened to the whale song again. It seemed more musical and calm. Singable, so I did. I sat between the singers and the drummers with my ear to hydrophone speaker. It seemed that we were all jamming in perfect synch – whales and humans. For a while I was sure I heard the Satchmo of whales crooning along with Windcloud our 83 year old song shaman…The boat sailed on. Those of us above water grew more musical and prayerful in the way of united minds. A family of whales - mama, big papa and baby came close and gave us a royal performance of breaching that went on and on. The boat load of humans sang an extended Hawaiian song in multiple harmonies spiced with calls and cries from those of us who could no longer contain ourselves in song; three women danced an impromptu hula on the front deck; their bright sarongs swaying in the breeze. The whales all breached together, then they breached one by one. Baby showed us how it was just learning to breach and daddy did double spirals like an extremely large spinner dolphin (that was impressive). They breached in pairs; they did side shimmy breaches then straight up and show us your belly breaches. They just kept on breaching as we sang and sounded and sailed with the wind. After an intoxicatingly timeless now, we went our separate ways. So sorry, Japan and Norway, no more whale meat; no more blubber. Not for sale. People ate people once too. No one claims cannibalism as a cultural necessity do they? Cetaceans aren't meat any more than I am. Just go visit them. You'll see OceanSong (lyrics below)…was first written in response to the US Navy's request of the National Marine Fisheries for permission to use low frequency sonar underwater, thus blowing the acoustic apparatus of whales apart in the interests of 'national insecurity'. in 2000 we chartered a small plane from Maui and travelled with didgeridoo, drums and 15 voices to the hearings on Oahu. We listened with pride to the environmental lawyers, the scientists, whale watch cruise captains, kahunas (Hawaiians of knowledge and power), locals, mothers and kids, and then we shared a song backed by 5 chants representing the continents, with recorded whales doing backing vocals representing the oceans. That changed things in those rather sedate chambers! Local news that night depicted a wave (sorry about the pun) of eco-activism through music.

OCEANSONG

In the beginning was the word
And from that word
Life was heard
All that is
Born of sound
From the heavens to the oceans
To the gentle ground
Echoing everywhere
Singers of Earth, sun and Air
And the voice in the waters
the cetaceans
We are the choirs of creation

Dear Mr Military give us time
We'll help you find
Peace of mind
But the voice in the waters
is a joy so strong
We must protect the Ocean Song

We all know the difference when we hear
A song of love or a cry of fear
Four footed animals know to run
From the sounds of danger - a bomb or a gun
But how can the creatures of the oceans hide
If you broadcast your terror

so far and so wide

Dear Mr Military give us time
We'll help you find
Peace of mind
But the voice in the waters
is a joy so strong
We must protect the Ocean Song

With just our voices we've prayed and sung
The whales and the dolphins they hear and they come
It's not okay - you cannot claim
It's safe to play your dangerous game
We who sing we are the walking relations
of the great cetacean nation

Dear Mr Military give us time
We'll help you find
Peace of mind
But the voice in the waters is a joy so strong
We must protect the Ocean Song

Om namah shivaya om shanti om shanti om [xix]
oh way oh wayah way oh [xx]
ka moana na uhane [xxi]

11 ~ The Possum Prince

The day that the British royals named their much awaited baby boy was one of the coldest days we had during our first winter in Tasmania. We decided to go walking earlier than usual to catch what traces of sunlight might be found amongst the mists and swirling chill rising from the river. About halfway into our very brisk walk I saw up ahead what looked like a dropped jacket.

It was a possum lying on her back. Yet another victim of cars moving at speeds to which marsupials, after 30 million years of slow paced living, have not yet adapted. The roads here are littered with beautiful, furry corpses. The crows grow fatter as the cars go faster. But something about this one caught my eye – her pouch was slightly open and I bent down to see a tangle of little claws and paws moving about.

I found myself improvising a marsupial caesarean. Gently pushing at the edge of the pouch on the far outer edges with my hand inside wrapped around the baby, I very carefully attempted to extract it without injury. A balance between gentleness and effectiveness; the pouch was stiff and cold; the baby needed to get out. Fast. I will always remember removing the long nipple from his mouth. (I have since learned it is better to cut the nipple and leave it in its mouth). He was almost completely frozen - chill as a little fish; naked with eyes not yet open but writhing about with that determination that life bestows upon its infants. I held him in my closed hands as we walked rapidly back to the car. In the icy winds David wrapped his cashmere scarf around my hands and I blew open mouthed hot breath into the space where the little body seemed to take forever to warm up. But he kept on writhing – more and more as he thawed out. By the time we got home he was less cold; his little tail was wrapped around one of my fingers and a tiny, soft-clawed paw was clutching another. Marsupial instincts I did not know I possessed took over – I tucked this handful of possum against my belly and covered it all with my jumper. Neither of us was warm enough though so I temporarily placed him into a sock while I donned some layers of silk knit and cashmere – the warmest combination I know. He made some amazingly loud sneezy, snuffly type noises for such a small creature, making it quite clear that the sock was not where he wanted to be. Once held again between my belly and my softest, warmest sweater he became calm.

It took a while to get through to the locally known wild animal carer, but eventually we found ourselves driving up to what is possibly the cosiest little stone castle on the planet. We were greeted by a tiny woman with a big heart and an OAM awarded for her services to wildlife in Northern Tasmania. As soon as we arrived Lorraine de Weys bustled us all into her warm-as-toast living room, then disappeared , emerging soon with a perfectly baby-possum-sized bag made of flannel, warmed it by the woodstove and tucked him in, giving him a couple of kisses on his head as she did so. Those kisses made it clear to me that he was in the best of hands. She then secreted him competently under her jumper, somehow securing him there so that unlike me, she still had two hands to function with. I could learn a lot from this woman, I thought as she brought out a kitchen scale, weighing first the bag and then the possum. "Seventy four grams; he's a boy." she informed us, which was great because David had already named him George. "Oh," she said, "I had one once which was only 46 grams at first and he made it. This little fella'll be OK; royal prince, huh?"

She then gave us a glimpse of two of her orphan wombats - each tucked into fluffy pink, baby-wombat-sized pouches. Wilshy (or won't she survive) the girl and Fred, the boy, though both vastly bigger than George and newly furred with eyes (somewhat sleepily) open, will remain with her for two years she told us. There were other wombats and a couple of padmelons (a bit like miniature kangaroos) living outdoors along with a big cockatoo who was making a huge noise; each one rescued from the wild animal carnage that occurs all over Tasmanian roads.

As we left we both felt a small miracle had occurred, but I couldn't bring myself to call until three days later because that little body had been so cold and it took so long, both to warm him and then to get food into him. I was not at all sure that such a vulnerable little creature could make it. "Oh George is doing great." said Lorraine, "He's drinking perfectly (not all of them do) peeing and pooing as good babies should and then back into his pouch with a hot water bottle by the fire to sleep till his next feeding. He's lucky," She said. "If you warm them too quickly or feed them when they are cold, they die. He's doing just fine." She knew so much about these precious little creatures. I know many Aussies learn to do this. It's one of the things I love about this country.

Of course, there was more to this than meets the eye. I did not rescue George, George rescued me. I was on the brink of despair for humanity...the refugee crisis, the news mantra of worldwide abuses, warfare, cruelty, hunger, climate change, and species extinction– oh you name it, this planet is suffering from it and I was feeling it all as one sometimes does after excessive media exposure. What is the point? It's hopeless... the place from where at times sincere prayer is forced to emerge - even from those of us who know too much to personalize the vast forces of existence. This was the kind of struggle going on in my soul as I walked that chilly riverside... 'I don't know who I'm praying too, but help us all anyway; give me some kind of a sign, a direction PLEASE'. And suddenly in my path is a creature that, like the planet, looks as if he has almost no hope of survival. Had David and I walked at our usual time a few hours later, this little guy would have been already dead. Even when we found him we both felt the faintness of his chances. But neither of us had any hesitation in doing whatever was possible for him. David had never worn that cashmere scarf before that day. (He'd owned it for years). What made us go out early? What is that force of life? We just did what we could, steeling ourselves for the possibility of another little dead body to deal with. David no doubt was preparing to dry some more of Jaiia's tears.

There have been countless dead possums on the roads since we arrived, but I never saw one splayed out on her back like that. Had she somehow made her pouch visible before she died? I can't help feeling that she did one of those heroic mother things in her last moments...thus saving her baby and teaching me that ultimate lesson of life:

Never give up.

This planet might look like it is beyond saving but it isn't. Love, the practical kind that is willing to wake up through the night to warm hot water bottles and marsupial infant formula for months and years at a stretch; that is the kind of love we need in these times. Each of us with our own special threads of loving kindness can co-create a web to gently hold this incredible planet and the amazingly beautiful life forms it contains.

We are all one family on this earth now. We humans have interfered with all species' habitats. It would be wonderful if we would all slow down when we are driving at night. We do it in human residential areas, why not for the animals? They were here before us. Some months after this I found myself driving through forested lands after midnight. One small animal showed itself on the road as we were starting out. I slowed down. Had I driven at normal country speeds I would have hit at least five nocturnal animals that night. They simply have no clue about highways and cars. And then there is this hit and run mentality. If your car does hit an animal, couldn't you stop and see if it is actually dead? Why should it lie in agony because of our impatience or our shame? If it is alive it needs a vet and if it is dead, then check and see: is there new life hidden in a pouch? There are some wonderful people like Lorraine ready and willing to raise the orphans of our highways.

Post script: About 10 days later, Lorraine called me. She was very sad. We had lost little George. It is no easy task to raise wild animal babies especially after the trauma that they experience so close to their mothers' deaths. But we had given him warmth and love to honour his short but precious life. And George gave me the gift of his journey. There are others who do make it. Most do not. This just highlights the message that nature repeats over and over again. Forests, trees, animals, babies, humans, health, bio-diversity, war...

Prevention is better than cure.
Tasmania is the road kill capital of the world.
Some 2 million animals dies on the roads here each year.
that means an animal loses its life every 30 seconds
Humans have a tendency to get used the horror of this carnage on the roads if they see it often enough. But if one has ever tried to replace the care that an animal mother gives her babies, one quickly sees these deaths as the absolute tragedy that they are.
Can we drive a little slower at night?
Is it so hard to live a little more kindly and listen to our own almost extinct instincts? Our world is still so incredibly beautiful. Every choice we make can help to keep it that way.

Tiny little smudge of fur
  How I wonder what you were
  Possum, quoll or wallaby?
  How could you ever possibly
  know to stop and look both ways
  or that a car would end your days
  The joey tucked inside your pouch
  can never cry out 'help' or 'ouch!'
  In thirty million years of peace
  you did not evolve for roads like these
  where humans driving speedy cars
  forget how vulnerable you are
  Perhaps one day their government might
  require them to slow down at night
  but till then only very few
  watch out from dusk till dawn
  for you.

13 ~ A Truly Remarkable Mammal

I was living in Topanga in California; a Bucky Fuller dome on a property quite aptly named 'Shangri La' as it is indeed a haven from the curious energetic time bomb that is Los Angeles. Some people thrive in the dream capital of the world. Others, like me, find it hard on the heart to be so surrounded by 'white man's idea of success' (Black Elk's phrase which has covered a multitude of crimes against nature since he first spoke it). Anyway I was there trying like everyone else to share my own personal dream: a rock opera written on behalf of a healthy planet.[xxii]

High above the multitudes, the property opens onto the dry, boulder strewn Malibu Hills where one can walk for silent miles overlooking the maelstrom below. One weekend I walked down into the Canyon for breakfast at a favourite spot. As I began my return walk, my moon flow began. I didn't give it too much thought. Just set off along the road that would lead back to the low lying mountain path towards home.

Suddenly three dogs were attacking me from behind. Apparently the unexpected moon flow was irresistible One of them bit through my jeans drawing blood. To my own satisfaction I turned into a raging Kali (the Hindu goddess of destruction) and turned snarling and roaring to chase them all home to where a door opened. A hand emerged, dragging the dogs in, and then the door slammed in my face.

So much for my injured leg. The raging Kali now reverted back into a somewhat shaken bleeding woman with a long way to walk home over the hills. Needless to say I survived, with my leg more intact than my faith in human nature.

The next week, no longer on my moon, I walked off into the mountains again – one has to get back on the horse – although this time, I avoided the suburbs and stayed amongst the high desert trails. Taking a small long abandoned path, I was walking into unknown terrain when something told me to stand very still. I stopped. Ahead of me I saw a marvellous boulder that looked like a large cat staring out over the misty valleys. As I stood watching, the boulder slowly turned its head and looked at me with eyes of greenish grey. We stood, gazing at one another for a timeless time…it felt like 15 minutes; it was probably less. I noticed its paws were big for its body and rather softly furred. Whatever it was, it was larger than a Doberman; it was not fully grown…in a season or two it would be daunting. Even now, had we shared anything less than mutual respect, this creature

exuded quite another kind of power than those three snarly
suburban dogs…

Eventually, still staring at one another, we both backed away.
The big cat went down the hill into the scrub while I went home
to explore what I had seen on a friend's computer. No…it was
not a bobcat it didn't have stripes and it was considerably bigger
with a long graceful tail.

It was a mountain lion.

Funny the difference one week can make. Domestic dogs
generally seem to reflect the consciousness of their owners.
Later I walked that way and saw signs stuck into their lawn that
had been stolen from the county: 'dogs must be kept on leashes'
and 'no dogs' – obviously these people saw their dog pack as a
local joke.

The mountain lion, however, was one of the high points of my
time in LA. Nobility and quiet grace. Rare to find such qualities
in a teenager in that town…

You will note, however, that attempting to engage it with sound
was the farthest thing from my instinctive mind.

14 ~ The Shadow ...
... & The Warriors of Peace

Having written about some of the most moving and beautiful moments in my life with animals, I have inevitably encountered a variety of situations both locally and worldwide that were anything but beautiful. The animal kingdom is crying out to be heard. But since I promised at the beginning of this book not to focus on the negative I am challenged: Just as it would have been inappropriate to write about the richness of Jewish culture during the years of the holocaust without also addressing the atrocity, so I cannot in conscience complete this book without speaking on behalf of animal rights. We need a United Species[xxiii] rather like the UN. Not that anything we do will instantly stamp out animal abuses any more than the UN can stop those inflicted upon humans by other humans, but at least there would be world standards to uphold. Just as sanctions are delivered upon rogue nations[xxiv] so such a body could be empowered to require decency in the treatment of animals until we globally awaken to the uncomfortable truth that exploitation of animals for our economic gain is as morally reprehensible as slavery. Of course, even now, human slavery abounds. Patience is a crucial attribute for those of us bent upon social change, even now as we appear to be living within the proverbial 11th hour. In the meantime we vote daily with our dollar and as more people loudly refuse to buy the products of cruelty the more quickly will we see kinder treatment worldwide as a basic standard towards innocent creatures.

"The greatness of a nation and its moral progress can be judged by the way its animals are treated." (Ghandi)

My only comment on that memorable quote would be (with all due respect and allowing for translators' mishaps) the pronoun 'its'. I do not see that animals belong to anyone or to any nation – at least not until they are given equal rights and the vote.

We are all in this together. Over six billion animals a year are slaughtered for meat in the US alone. And no one who does the first level of research can pretend those animals are treated decently in the process. Torture not just death is common amongst all species being exploited for food, fur, ivory, cosmetics, medicines or anything else. The same industrial machine dominates the dairy industry basically producing 'tortured cow juice' of varying degrees of toxicity depending on whether you buy organic or otherwise, while the treatment of animals worldwide under the banner of 'science' is almost incomprehensible. That creatures from the great apes capable of sign language and computer use along with profound social skills and self-awareness,(see endnote xii)) to fluffy little bunny rabbits are still submitted to lives of ongoing physical and psychological cruelty is a factor to be considered in every cosmetic or pharmaceutical that one chooses to use. And our universities and psychology research departments are all heavily implicated in this ongoing nightmare.

 We will never be happy on this planet as long as we treat others – of our own or any species - without the kindness and respect that we all wish for ourselves. It is a simple equation. No matter how well trained is our conscious mind, our hearts are linked to all beings. Denials and justification may act like oil upon troubled waters at the surface, but if truth is not lived, troubles ferment in the depths. Heart disease, environmentally exacerbated illnesses like cancer and pulmonary illness, intestinal inflammation etc. are not so different from revolution and war amongst nations; all have emotional and mental foundations along with whatever physical components are discovered and defined as 'causes'. Eating the by-products of torture and slavery is bound to impact our health whether or not we are conscious of the connection.

for a while I had some difficulties with a friend's Facebook posts emerging from the militant vegan movement of Israel. It seemed that they were denying the atrocities of Gaza on their doorstep, but I learned that these activists believe that violently produced foods generate violence in the people and that by eating compassionately we create a foundation for world peace…maybe even peace in the Middle East!

Let me add here that I am not an absolute vegan. I care about where my food is sourced and at times I compromise, just as I do every time I drive a car or fly in a plane. I have yet to find a way to live on this planet in absolute integrity…which keeps me humble. I am just another creature stumbling around on Mother Earth searching for a way through the shadows and the light, doing the best I can.

PERFECTLY HUMAN

I'm not a perfect human
but I'm perfectly human
I have strived all my life for perfection
so much correction
to make myself more of
what I was sure that
a perfect human ought to be

Do you know what that might mean?
Do you understand the difference between
being a perfect human and a perfectly human being?

Well it means that we've a stake in every mistake
that us imperfect humans ever make

How many children do you see
who get to grow feeling loved and feeling free
yet isn't that most of what us imperfect humans
really need?

Well I'm not a perfect human
but I'm perfectly human
and you man - yes you
are you perfectly human too ?[xxv]

135

There are levels of existence where Newtonian physics – the cause and effect version of reality – simply does not hold true. Einstein once stated that the only reason for time is so that everything doesn't happen all at once. It is a kind of convenience. Without time, there is no sequential 'cause' leading to 'effect'; all is simultaneous. Our kindness, our cruelty, our honesty or otherwise and our health and quality of life are all one event. This can be very difficult to grasp. As one physicist put it 'Anyone who tells you that they understand relativity is probably lying'. Eventually though, just as the Galilean version of the solar system (the earth moving around the sun, not vice versa) became obvious truth, so the quantum realm will become part of the education of all children. At a sub atomic level particle can become wave and wave can become particle. In that sense, our thoughts and our feelings *are* our flesh and they are shared with every cell in existence; especially and most immediately with those of the mother planet. We rise or fall together, our choices creating our destiny both as individuals and as co-creators of *this* tiny part of the universe at the very least. At a macrocosmic level we may be far more significant that our culture could handle. Because if we were ever to awaken en masse to how rare and extraordinary is life on earth, then all forms of slavery would become intolerable; the economics of scarcity would collapse and we would take our place within the natural world, both humbled and exalted. Something new and completely different would inevitably emerge.

Something beyond our tame old same old dreams.

We may not like that our own species is upsetting the balance in the exquisite, delicate web of life that we call home, but unless we are living naked in a cave eating wild foods and walking everywhere, we are all participants. The way I see it is this: We are responsible; we are not to blame. There is a difference: one attitude empowers, the other induces paralyses. So long as we reject what is going on by judging it as something happening outside of ourselves, we are impotent. Acceptance is a point of power. Admittedly it is a bridge, like forgiveness. Without rejection there is nothing to accept and without judgement there is nothing to forgive. As the Dalai Lama so succinctly puts it, compassion towards others is enlightened self-interest. That would include the 'perpetrators' as well as the 'victims'. Like I said – we are all in this together. At times that might seem like a burden. but in fact it is our only hope. As the prophets of many indigenous cultures keep trying to tell us, we *are* the ones we have been waiting for.

Can you handle that much response-ability? Can we do it together?

This world needs each one of us to stand in our own loving power - whatever that means for each individual. For some like Amma Ji, the hugging saint, that is a world-encompassing embrace that includes a massive outreach of compassionate action towards those of us living in the helplessness of poverty. For others like Captain Paul Watson and his roguishly courageous Sea Shepherd eco-pirates it is a warrior's stance protecting the animals in our oceans. Then there is the legal scholar, Steven Wise and his fellow lawyers, Natalie Prosin, the executive director of the Nonhuman Rights Project (Nh.R.P.), and Elizabeth Stein, a New York based animal-law expert, who have begun the crucial and patient steps towards 'civil rights for animals' in the courts of the US.[xxvi] Some work to protect ecosystems, some are working on alternative energy and some are raising well-loved and consciously educated children…Most of the world's heroes are unseen and unacknowledged, working invisibly, step by tiny step to sort out whatever piece of this puzzle is theirs to deal with. It is safer that way as the cult of celebrity feeds off its own self-created monsters.

I invite you after reading this book to do whatever your heart requires of you to uncover your true potential in this critical time in human existence. According to the ancient Vedic scriptures of India, we are living in the Kali Yuga, the darkest of all ages. and yet it is said to be the time of greatest light because in this age it is easier than in any other for an individual to attain enlightenment. An active shift in consciousness could, even now, turn around the damage we have done to the biosphere. The rapidity with which dead rivers recover once they are left unpolluted is extraordinarily encouraging. We are capable of transformation. I know this because I have directly experienced it, both personally and amongst a wonderful, if motley collection of sentient beings, not all of them human.

There is a tiny drop of honey on my kitchen counter right now and there is an ecstatic little circle of ants celebrating my clumsiness. I have a choice. I can wipe them all 'away' and keep my kitchen clean and tidy, or I can turn a blind eye and risk my kitchen becoming ant central for the local environs…or perhaps I can think outside the box and find another option – one that will probably require a little patience. I will not tell you what I choose. But I must warn you that these and other time consuming issues do become part of existence once we drop our hubris and recognise our humble place amongst all beings! And in the bigger picture one might consider: are we the ants by the honey smear, or are we the sponge wielding housekeeper?

What would really clean up our environment most effectively at this point? I believe there is nothing more important than compassionately reducing population density. How? All statistics prove that the education of women is the single most effective form of birth control. And my own experience amongst teachers of sexual consciousness tells me that a massive upleveling of sexual education for both men and women would go a long way towards reducing the ubiquity of sexual violence worldwide.

More wanted children and less unwanted would lead us to a very different world future with room and resources for our own species and all the others with whom we share this magnificent world. I realise that this is not the only issue, and many great thinkers will cite free clean energy as the ultimate game changer. But as a woman, trusting my left brain/ right brain synthesis, commonly known as intuition, and adding to it my 'womb wisdom' I see this as fundamental to the creation of healthier world. Mine is a relative truth, but one that is pertinent to my planetary family of all species.

And it is to you my loved ones, most of whom will never know me, that I dedicate this book:

∞

140

Acknowledgements ~

First and foremost I wish to thank our planet ~ Mother Earth,

Gaia ~ which by any name at all remains the single most important source of everything other than sunlight and cosmic energies that are as yet incomprehensible to the author.

Thank you each animal who has graciously shared your sweet

magic with me; each one of you has treated me with incredible gentleness, kindness and humour. Such an honour...

Thank you Tui Allen, for the artwork that graces the cover.

Author also of the beautiful and profound book 'Ripple'. A mythologically 'true story' about how a dolphin brought music into our universe. Tui contributed her time and artwork so that animals can have one more quiet voice speaking on their behalf.

Thanks also to those rare humans who have been capable of honouring the journey that has involved the seeming insanity of, for example spending hours feeding a sick bee with honey on the tip of my finger rather than working for the global corpocracy. That would include my beloved husband, David along with all those who have shared parts of this life with me either as friends, housemates or partners along the path.

Thank you to all my teachers of sound – especially the late Mechtild Harkness and Sister Mary Gabriel, Joseph Mani (still with us!) and the humpback whales whose winters are spent in the waters off Maui Hawaii.

Thank you to all those who devote incredible amounts of their lives to caring for injured, orphaned or endangered animals worldwide. it is people like you who give me hope for the future of humanity. Thank you to the animal activists worldwide. We need you!

There are some photos herein that I have found on the web. Where possible I have sent requests for permission to use these images but so far few replies. If you find your image here, please contact me. I wish to do this right with you. Thank you!

Thank you to my mother, a uniquely heart centred human who has been loved and trusted by pretty much every animal and every sentient being who has ever met her and could bear to be in the presence of childlike innocence. If it is true that one has to become like a child to enter the kingdom of heaven, then my mother Eve has a guaranteed ticket. She left this world on January 12th 2018. Her life, as my brother put it remains "a mystical poem". A poem of loving kindness to all beings.

xxvii

Meetings with Remarkable Animals ©2018 Jaiia Earthschild
All rights reserved

All song lyrics quoted are ©2017 Jaiia Earthschild All rights reserved and the songs maybe streamed or downloaded at http://jaiiaearthschild.wixsite.com/earthschild

Endnotes ~

some of which are stories unto themselves…enjoy!

---

[i] By 'animals' I am referring to all creatures that are not human, mineral or plant…although at times, the demarcation lines do get a little flimsy.

[ii] 'I Clitoris – the Autonomous woman's guide to the healing and Awakening of her Sacred Sexual Nature' and 'Moon Mythstories'' almost self-published!

[iii] To quote Ricky Gervais

[iv] ©1989 Jaiia Earthschild from the album 'The Children of Eve"

[v] This picture was taken on the very earth day and yes the bird is on my finger although invisible here...the next pic I tried to blow it up so you could see the bird...good luck! It is the only visible record we have

[vi] yes see! that is a bird wild and fearless, sitting on my finger!

[vii] sadly these lorikeets by the family veranda are poorly represented in black and white. Had I printed them in their lavish color, this book would be too costly to sell

[viii] Thanks to Eve for this photo and the others of me n' da boids

[ix]see note yii - this guy is golden with vivid green eyes!

[x] *Chapter 6* - Cat-Addendum

I did say that it is not my intention to write about domesticated animals in this particular book. I am including a 'cat' in this rather extended endnote is because it is inextricably linked to a certain golden bee with emerald green eyes. I am of the opinion that the cat is the only animal to have successfully domesticated the human, but that is another story.

Re "Bee-attitudes" 12 years later... Shortly before our marriage, we moved into a cedar house high up on the slopes of Haleakala, the mountain that is at least half of Maui. The farm gate opened onto the ranch lands of Oprah Winfrey. We could see six islands from our lanai (veranda). Some months earlier I had been summarily adopted by a glorious infant white tiger, an Egyptian Mau kitten named Treasure and we were one happy little family. A couple had to abandon their little golden tiger kitten – who was pretty much the same age as Treasure but who was, by breed considerably smaller. She was left petrified in the apartment below. I asked Treasure to be kind to her as she had also known the terrors of orphanhood, having been rescued by yours truly from under the wheels of my car in the middle of a very busy road some months earlier. Touchingly, Treasure would wait outside the downstairs cat door until she was invited

in and then proceed to teach the little kitten all about being a
Cat. The little one had never set foot outdoors before and their
friendship together was delightful to watch – chasing butterflies
in the veggie garden; discovering catnip (!) and generally being
as joyful as young cats are in a country setting. The little cat
began to visit us upstairs more and more often and was very
clearly not at all interested in returning downstairs at night;
reports came of head banging against the cat door and vomiting
in emotional anguish. Treasure discovered jealousy as she
realised that her downstairs neighbour was planning to move in.
The little cat was ingenious and extraordinarily agile. One night,
looking from my bed into a vase of flowers, I noticed that a
large voluptuous chrysanthemum was sporting whiskers and two
furry ears. This was one determined little feline. Well why not?
We were in love, the food was organic and I am a devoted
animal lover. And besides, there were subtle signs that made me
wonder. Both cats sported the identical markings in different
colours as if painted by the same artist. Treasure was having
none of it and took me out to the mountainside to commune
severely about how Utterly Inappropriate it would be to have
Two Cats when One is obviously Plenty. There came a time
when we had to make a radical escape from this house, it having
been painted with a neurotoxic cedar preservative that also froze
our nervous systems and as we fitted our few belongings into the
truck to leave, our little golden friend somehow found her way
onto my lap, looking soulfully up at me with her intense emerald
eyes. At that moment something clicked. I had seen those eyes

before. When we arrived at our new and very temporary miniature castle, I pulled out my treasure bag. I told David about the golden bee. He was only just getting to know me to be what I suppose some would like to call 'a witch' (I am not but it does run in the family). At the end of the story, I used a knife to open the by now completely sealed sarcophagus and there inside lay the uncorrupted body of my bee friend. Only the eyes were gone. They were now looking at us from our new and ecstatically happy cat friend, who was by this time defying gravity by tearing up the walls and somersaulting on the high timber beans in delight. Her fur, when rubbed the wrong way proved to be the same exact colour as the bee. Since her outer fir looked rather like a cinnamon swirl, she was renamed that day: "Ninja B. Muffin". Treasure took some time to adapt but eventually the cats became once again best friends despite much sibling rivalry.

Six years later when it came time for us to move internationally, I communed with each of them. It was a long and terrible journey they faced in the underbelly of a jet with a month of quarantine upon arrival in a strange country with ticks and snakes and other things for which they had neither immunity nor ancestral learning., There is a simple way to commune with animals using picture thinking. My own highly language oriented brain has no trouble translating animals' responses so quickly that I barely get time to see the images. When I asked her about immigrating Muffin's first clear response was 'Oh no, I don't want to do that'. I was shocked and found myself in paroxysms of grief. Then one day as I was writing, she came up to my keyboard and rolled over on her head across the keys. She had always done this to express her passionate love and enthusiasm. After she was finished, there was curious line of .type, so I enlarged it to see what she had written. I called David to come upstairs as a witness. (He has always called me 'Jai'). This was her love letter to me, untouched by human hands:

jijijiijijijijijijijijijijijijijijijijijijijijijijijijijijijijijijijikkkkkk∞cccccxxxxxxx
xxxxxxxxxxxxxxxxxxxxxxxxxxxxxxxxxxxxxx

"Ji (Jaiia) – k (thousands) - infinity (I have signed my name with this symbol since I was a child) - c (hundreds) - x (kisses)

Yes, yes I know that this was not an act of conscious typing. But how many cats do you know who write with such clear symbolism? I recommend the book *Why Cats Paint* should you find this issue to be bothersome.

I called various wise women about my dilemma. One of the wisest pointed out that she was obviously an enlightened genius and I did not need to worry about her, she will love me forever. And I have a love letter from a creature who has pretty much proved to me that the transmigration of souls is possible, even if it is rare. I will repeat that in general, I find domestication (of animals *and* women) to be a serious moral issue…and cats are almost as damaging in the wild as the humans who abandon them there. But since I am sure there must be countless stories about them in all their quirky glory, perhaps the next volume of this series will have to include a few extraordinary cat tails (!)…

[xi] Many times I have been bee-friended - but never with a camera (they usually are sitting on my finger), so for the first time I took pencil to paper for this bee in flight...

[xii] Thanks to Eve Downs for saving this scary critter for 30 years pickled in alcohol and thanks to Anthony Downs for the photo

[xiii] The Hawaii-based man who took this photo and kindly gave me his permission to use it some years ago has disappeared from my radar. thank you! It was exactly this spider on exactly this kind of wall.

[xiv] I have tried for months to find the origin of this gorgeous photo - thank you whoever you are!
[xv] Available on the CD earthSchild or to stream: https://soundcloud.com/jaiia-david-e-t/catch-the-midnight-sky?in=jaiia-david-e-t/sets/earthschild

[xvi] Thanks to Bryce Groark for permission to use this photo

[xvii] thank you to http://www.australianbushbirds.info for this delightful photo
Chapter 8:[xviii] The US navy later exempted itself from the marine mammal protection act for two years while they staged military exercises (full scale war type) in Hawaiian waters, deploying sonar ten to one billion times louder than that which caused the mass stranding of whales and subsequent disappearance of all whales of that type in the Bahamas some years previously. California successfully chased the navy and its

exercises out of their waters with law suits. At the time of writing mid-range frequency sonar continues to be deployed. Between this and all the other noise pollution in the oceans, the melting of the ice caps, over-fishing, plankton reduction, ocean desertification and the International Whaling Commission trying to force the return of commercial whaling, it looks like a tough time to be a whale. Now krill oil has become the new superfood. Frankly humanity, could we perhaps leave the krill for the whales to eat? I hear that fish oil works just as well, and the whales need all the nourishment they can get. Their message to us? "Save the humans"

[xix] Sanskrit: translation: *I bow to Shiva the destroyer - the inner self that remains intact when everything ends*

[xx] Native American chant

[xxi] Hawaiian: *Spirit of the oceans*

[xxii] 'OurStory' Jaiia Earthschild 2002

[xxiii]acknowledgements to Jim Loomis for this idea

[xxiv] unless they happen to be economically significant nations to which so called democracies are in massive debt, at which point denial rules. Cumulative debt is symptomatic of a loss of power. As anyone whose home is in foreclosure to the banksters of this world will tell you, it is difficult to require integrity of one's creditors.

[xxv] From the song *Perfectly Human* by Jaiia Earthschild and David Techau ©2014

[xxvi] From the article - *"The Rights of Man and Beast?"* By Charles Siebert, NYT April 23, 2014: "… As recently as 10 years ago Wise's effort would have been laughed out of a courtroom. What has made his efforts viable now, however, is in part the advanced neurological and genetic research, which has shown that animals like chimpanzees, orcas and elephants possess self-awareness, self-determination and a sense of both the past and future. They have their own distinct languages, complex social interactions and tool use. They grieve and empathize and pass knowledge from one generation to the next. The very same attributes, in other words, that we once believed distinguished us from other animals. Wise intends to wield this evidence in mounting the case that his clients are "autonomous beings," ones who are able, as Wise defines that term, "to freely choose, to self-determine, to make their own decisions without acting from reflex or innate behavior." He sees these abilities as the minimum sufficient requirement for legal personhood."

[xxvii] photo of my mother, Eve Downs with her great granddaughter, Maisie taken by one of the family…thanks!

Printed in Great Britain
by Amazon